Introduction

Hello to whoever is reading this. This is my first ever book and I have worked extremely hard on it. It has probably been the hardest thing I've worked on since my GCSE's.

I have written this book and released it because I feel I am in a good position in my life where I can be on TV and have some sort of a platform where I can talk about things that matter and people can actually listen to me.

You will be utterly shocked after reading this book as there are not that many things that people know about me at all! I have been through a lot, but then we all have and I am not here to write about a sad story or tell a sad story about part of my life. I am writing about how we can get through certain issues and in doing so see how we can achieve our biggest dreams.

I am 23, I still have a lot to learn but I am very smart and I have experienced a lot in my life…

I have experienced what most people have, heartbreak, loss, alcohol abuse, bullying, behaviour disorders but most of all I have experienced love and happiness.

I am super nervous having this book out for anyone to buy and read but, to be honest, if this book can save my life then it could save yours too.

What you are about to read and learn is all true. I haven't lied about anything. I have been really honest, maybe too honest.

Due to the honest nature of this book certain people's names have been changed to protect their identity.

Enjoy x

CHAPTER ONE
Pre-school

Hi! I am Ronan, Ronan Rice. Can't believe I have actually written a book. Well, this is my first sentence and hopefully after reading the whole thing you will instantly fall in love with me, and hopefully ask me out on a date, haha.

This is literally something I have always wanted to do. I have grown up not really in the limelight or spotlight because, let's face it, I wasn't really "famous". But growing up wasn't really easy at all. Let's go back to where it all began!

I was clearly a magical gift from GOD when my beautiful mummy found out
she was expecting me back in the 90s. I was born on the 27th of October 1994, nearly killing my very poorly mum. I didn't quite have the normal birth. Apparently my mum almost died. She was rushed into hospital a few days after I was born with internal bleeding, or something serious along those lines. We were separated for a while but I managed to stay in hospital with her after she was saved. Thank GOD she is okay now though! You will come to see that she plays a big part in my life.

I was raised in the Old Model Farm area of Downpatrick, Northern Ireland. I lived in a small house, with my mum Trisha, my darling sister Laura, and my dad... Well I thought he was my dad. Until some spiteful, interfering person told me he wasn't my real dad. Yeah, very confusing. My real dad left my mum and I when I was one year old. Very sad, but honestly I was so young, I never knew him. I don't even have any photos of him and I together so to be honest he doesn't really exist to me.

I feel a bit sorry for my sister Laura. She was the first born, and she had a good time with Trish before I came along. She goes on that I ruined her childhood, but I know deep down she literally loves me just as much as I love her. I remember back in the 90's Mum was always away early in the morning for work, and God knows where Dad was. Laura always woke me up in the morning and made me cheese on toast, the wee cheese slices, the really cheap ones, not real cheese. Then after our breakfast was made we went into the living room and watched *Saved By The Bell*. I remember always taking hissy fits because I wanted *Honey I Shrunk The Kids* on instead of boring old *Saved By The Bell*.

I am pretty sure my sister raised me as much as my mum did. Thanks Sis. She was super cool. I remember her always going out with her friends and I was at home playing with mum's high heels and dresses, haha. Laura and I were always bickering. We did everything together, and she did everything for me. I remember when I was super young, about 4 or 5, and I was in the bath. Mum and Dad were watching a real dramatic movie, and didn't want to miss anything because back in the day you couldn't really pause live TV. Anyway back to the story.... I was in the bath, and they were watching a movie, so Laura had to come up and take me out of the bath. The true jelly legs that she is, she dropped me down the stairs, head first, into a wall. I am pretty sure she hurt her leg that night, because she was walking weird for weeks but even then it was all about me! I still remind her to this day that she almost killed me, drama drama.

I knew from a young age that I always wanted to be a star. I remember at my mum and dad's wedding, everyone was loving life, watching me on the stage, dancing in my cute Barney PJs. Many people always dream of having an amazing job, then when they get older they go for something different. But with me, I have always stayed with the same dream, to be a star.

Being a star for me is like everybody loving you. I wanted to make people laugh, cry, and be happy, even all those years ago. I wanted the whole package!

I also wanted Barbies, but never got them. I would have to sneak up to my cousin's house to play with her Barbies.

My childhood indoors was amazing. Mum wouldn't let us out at an early age. We always had to stay inside where it was safe. It's when I was allowed out of the garden things turned into shit.

Being able to play outside of your house, with people who you thought were your friends, sounded amazing. But literally it was only the start of the constant bullying and heartbreak.

There was a big field beside my house, where all the kids would go and light fires, play with stones, and run around together playing whatever imaginary game they played. I was a normal kid. Well, what I thought was normal. Prancing around in Trisha's high heels every halloween as a witch, until my dad took them off me, and threw them in a bin. What an idiot.

I was different than the other kids. I knew that even then. Everyone was playing with all these Pokemon games, and

Action Men. All I wanted to do was play Barbies, or to play Mummy and Daddies. I always wanted to be the Mummy.

There was never that one friend who ever had my back in that field, especially when things got rough.

The older ones came into the field and chased after us. I was the slowest runner and fell. I was hit, spat at, picked on for being "gay". Me being so young I had no idea what that was. I was only a child. I think now that I am an adult I should really have had that choice to be gay or straight. I didn't need people to tell me who or what I was at such a young age. Then I think, if I had an easier childhood…. would I be straight?

The good thing about that field was that I could always go back home again. Back to my comfort zone.

I was able to have sleepovers in Nanny Dee's every weekend, which took my mind off anything that was bothering me. She would always be so cool and let me watch a horror movie, and never made me close my eyes! I loved horror movies, they were the best! I think one of my favourites would have to be *Sleepy Hollow*. That was a terrifying movie to watch at my age. I couldn't stop thinking about the wee freak with no head coming into my room to kill me during the middle of the night.

Thank God it was just a movie.

My Nanny Dee will always have her own wee place in my heart. She has taught me so many things in life that I can never forget. She also made me learn how to use a hoover, which is a really good lesson to know for the future. Take note kids, I now know what's important!

My childhood wasn't all bad. I always had some sister time. We would run around the house together with fake guns and wee targets, and try to shoot each others targets until we had no ammo left. It was such a cool game, I wish I remembered what it was called. What I do remember was every single Saturday my Nanny Dee, Laura, Geraldine, Mummy, and of course myself, would do a trip down the town and go shopping. Everything was so cheap back then as well. I was always so excited because we would be able to go into Eason's Shop which is now closed down - SAD TIMES. I would go into the shop every Saturday and buy a *Buffy The Vampire Slayer* comic, and some figures. I had at least 20 comics. I was really such a nerd if you think about it. I used to get so excited over superhero comics and action figures. (At least I had time off playing with Barbies.) Life was so easy back then, getting to run around the town and nobody had any idea who you were. You could wear whatever you want, say whatever you want. Look wherever you want.

Most weekends the whole extended family would come down to Nanny Dee's and play cards. It was a family tradition. Quite fun, but yet so annoying, as I had no idea how to play cards with the grown ups and I always felt left out. I would be in the living room playing with my cousins, while the grown ups were inside. I loved my cousins. I mostly played with Hayley and Corey. They are literally the coolest kids you will ever meet. They are both proper ginger which makes them even more cool! They are grown up now and still play around and joke around at family occasions. We will never grow up to be honest. Don't ever change kids.

My mum always took me to such cool places. I remember having long walks around the Quoile River, going to the cinema, having loads of good tasty food. My mum made everything possible for me to have a good childhood, she really did. She really worked her ass off trying to make me happy, and she still does. She used to work during the days, then work late evenings, sometimes up in Belfast. Mum and I would always walk past this beautiful old tree. Every time we walked by I would try and climb it. Each year I got older, the higher I would climb. I am still trying to get to the top. Its quite hard. It's a bit like my life really, always reaching for something more.

I will always respect my mum for that. Even though she could be having the worst day ever, or dealing with loads of stress, she would still put on a really good show to make me happy. And it always worked. I was always happy when I was around her. She is the rock that no one can replace. A mother's hug is warm and special, and yet so important. What I have learned is you never bite the hand that feeds you. I learnt that recently, and I will never forget it! This adulthood is hard work!

CHAPTER TWO
School

My mum and dad never seemed happy together. I don't know if I put a strain on their marriage, or maybe they just weren't happy. Did I become the problem child? I always heard them fighting or giving off. There was one horrible day when Dad went crazy and threw the dinner all around the house. I think witnessing something like that at such a young age would stay in my mind. Don't get me wrong, every family fights. But things were just so miserable. It wasn't fun.

Things just got more intense when it came to me starting school. I was bullied mostly everyday. I was so excited to start primary school because I always wanted to make new friends. I still look at the cheesy, smiling photographs of myself posing in the front garden with my new uniform, school bag and lunch box on show. I was beautiful!

I wanted real friends, friends who would be there for me and look after me. But instead I got the complete opposite. I hated primary school. Nobody ever wanted to sit beside me, except one guy, Peter, I loved him! We are still really good drinking buddies. He is super cool and very tall, with a cool beard! I remember things got so bad in primary school I had to pretend I liked football just to talk to my classmates.

Not all of my childhood was horrible. I do remember the amazing birthday parties my family planned for me. Bouncy castles, the amazing caterpillar cake, ugh - I need cake! That caterpillar cake still makes an appearance with all the other family members.

There was always something missing, and I didn't know what it was. Was there something inside me wanting to come out? Or was there always something bugging me? I really didn't know. But I was happy sometimes. I was happy the most when I was around my mummy, Nanny, and my amazing Auntie Geraldine - she is the BEST!

Coming home from school was sometimes fun because, if Dad wasn't home, I would get to run over to my Nanny Dee's house to play and do my homework. Geraldine, my Auntie, would always play *"What's The Time Mr Wolf"* in the hallway. I giggled so much. I hope to play that game with my kids someday. We are so close with Geraldine now that I am older, we get to talk about almost anything! Sometimes I overstep the line and bring up how many guys I have kissed, for example, then she stops the conversation! I love how I can now do this. It makes me want to scream out that your family can be your best support, never forget that.

My dad was always very weird when I wanted to go over to Nanny's. He would never let me go over if he was at home. Even when he was home he didn't even do anything with me anyway. I would just sit in my room playing with my teddies or later with my amazing dog, Keano, loved that dog!

I moved house when I was still in primary school. That's when I got Keano. We moved to a different estate, a bit further from Nannies. The years had moved on and I was no longer dressing up as witches, or pink power rangers, for halloween. I am pretty sure my dad shook all of that nonsense out of me before high school. Despite that I ended primary school on a high, knowing I will be going to a different school after the summer, and no one will ever have to bully me again. I could start over even though I would 100 percent miss my music teacher, Mrs Hagan, who let me sing *"My Heart Will Go On"* on the piano before leaving primary school. I will always remember how amazing she was.

I didn't want to go to any of the schools in Downpatrick, because I knew I get picked on for being "gay", and I still didn't know what that meant.

The summer was ending. Mum, once again, was rushing around finding the right uniform to wear. What fits, what doesn't fit. Since I was really skinny, nothing ever fitted me. I got my tonsils taken out the summer before, and I literally stopped eating because I always felt like I was going to choke. I lost a lot of weight before the first year in high school. I mostly binge watched the *Lizzie McGuire Movie* while eating ice cream all summer, while waiting for my throat to heal.

Today was the day I started big school. I was literally so excited. I am going to be going to HIGH SCHOOL! I am going to make new friends. Maybe find a girlfriend. Maybe join the school choir. Oh the excitement!

Mummy dropped me down to the bus station, along with my so called friends, who I went to primary school with. Of course they ignored me as soon as we got on the bus, because they knew other people through football and what not. I was sitting on my own.

Driving from Downpatrick to Crossgar, which is only 10-12 minute drive, felt like hours.

My mummy had tied my tie so tightly, I felt like I could hardly breathe. I had little skinny legs, my trousers looked so big on me. We finally got to the school where I saw a couple of older boys and girls standing by the railings, waiting for us to get off the bus. I was a bit worried. I didn't know why they were just standing there watching us. All us boys and girls got off the bus, and walked towards the doors. While I was walking towards the doors I noticed a girl who looked awfully familiar.... Did she live near me?

"Hello, welcome first years" said the older kids, as I realised they were here to look after us. We all got assigned our own mentors for the school year. "Hello my name is Mikey"...that was it. My stomach literally fell to the ground, and my heart started to beat really fast. What was the matter with me? Was I taking a stroke? Did I see a ghost?

Walking behind my mentor, Mikey, was the most thrilling walk of my life. Well, I thought it was the most thrilling walk, until I was on *MTV's Ex On The Beach Body SOS,* but we aren't talking about that yet! We are talking about my HIGH SCHOOL CRUSH!

Walking behind Mikey was amazing. The smell of his aftershave, the cute colours on his school bag, his nice spiked up hair, and his perfect smile. Every time he turned around to ask me if I was okay... I was more than okay. If this is what High School is going to feel like everyday please let me stay forever.

Now, let's talk about the canteen.... The food was okay, the curry was amazing. Other than that the other food was alright. I was sitting on a long table with all the lads. I wasn't fitting in already. No-one was talking to me. Was I maybe too shy?

My first day flew in and it was time to get back on the bus and head home. Mikey waved goodbye to me, I waved back.

Oh the butterflies.

The week went on with me following Mikey all around the school, eating the amazing curry, and enjoying my drama class. I felt so happy in drama class. Was this a sign of things to come? I can't really remember my drama teacher, but she was so nice. She always knew how to cheer me up when I was feeling a bit left out. But I've got to say there was also something about my Religious Studies teacher, Mrs Bell. Her smile could light up a whole room. I loved going to her class.

As the week went on I kept trying to fit into certain groups. The girls always laughed at me because I always wore a vest under my shirt. They always laughed about that. Don't know why it was funny. Then I found out why!

The first day of football.... The boy's locker rooms.... We all had to strip in front of each other in a cold, old, rusty shower room. Of course I never went into the showers, because I was always afraid in case they would beat me up, take my shorts off, or even worse.... I'd get a raging boner! Not one of the boy's were wearing vests. Why was I the only one wearing one. I got so much stick for wearing a silly vest, and it started a rumour around the school that I was actually wearing a bra!

I had such a shit second week in school, the teachers stopped bothering to help me fit in. My mentor wasn't really asking if I was okay anymore. Maybe I was a bit weird with him, after all he was my first real crush. After P.E class I went to the toilet to get changed, because I didn't want anyone to laugh at me for wearing a vest. Then it happened. My first ever situation with the twins. They were classed as the school bullies. Not only bullying me, but bullying others as well. I am not naming them, as I would probably get beat up again if they read this. But if you are reading this boys, haha look at me now!

I came out of my little bathroom stall, and they they were. "Ronan, you dropped your gay card". They pushed me to the ground and laughed. My clothes were covered in dirt and the wet piss from the floor. It was horrible, I just wanted to go home and get a cuddle of my mummy. It was so embarrassing that this was happening all over again. I thought High School was supposed to be fun.

The days went on. I was literally begging my mum to write sick notes so I didn't have to go to P.E class. I dreaded waking up in the mornings, knowing I had to face the bullies. Mostly everyone gets bullied in their life, I get it, but everyday is literally awful. Why me?

I hated being different. I hated going home pretending I had a good day when I really didn't. Most kids got home fast because they were so excited to tell their parents how amazing their day was but what did I have to rush home to and what did I have to tell? But enough of the depressing stories for now. It was the big day, last day before summer started!

So, I survived the first year! Well, just about. It was the last day before summer started and I was on the bus on the way home from school. The girl that kept walking past me on the bus every morning was sitting up front on her own. I just had to sit beside her and introduce myself. Yes that was very forward of me to do, but I literally had to! She was so familiar and I had to find out who she was! I picked up my school bag and my blazer and I made my way over to the front seat. All the time trying not to cause any scenes, because the bullies were still at the back of the bus, chanting some dumb shit. I sat down and said "Hi. Don't I know you?", she looked at me like I had three heads. She said very quietly "Yeah, didn't you go to the same nursery school as me?", I was like, "YES!".

CHAPTER THREE
Girls

Instant BOND! I had my first friend that was a girl! I was loving life! What a difference from before. Every day during the summer I would message her on *Bebo*. I knew she had other friends that would sit at the big long table in the canteen, across from me and the boys. I always wondered what it would be like to have a group of friends that were girls, and a group of friends in general! I would meet up with the girl who was named Gloria, pretty much my best friend! We did everything. We went shopping on Saturdays, we went to the cinema, and occasionally even went swimming! I felt like I could tell her almost anything about my life and not be ashamed of it.

She was so tiny and small, she was literally so cute. As the summer went on, I loved my life even more. Knowing I would be going back to school with a friend was amazing. A REAL FRIEND!

As much fun I was having there was always this voice in the back of my head about being gay. Was I gay? Was I meant to know at such a young age? Why do I still feel these questions going round and round in my head?

Summer was officially over and I wanted to get back into school! I got off the bus with Gloria, and I asked her very nicely if I could sit with her and her classmates during lunch… she said "I'll ask them". I actually know what they said as well, because they were never happy with having a guy in their group. There were 7 of them and they had such a strong tight bond, but there was no way I was having no for an answer. So

I literally rushed after class to get a seat in the canteen with them! The Girl Squad!

The Girl Squad consisted of; Laura, Jessica, Gloria, Lucy, Josephine, Naomi, and Aoife. Laura was the very pretty blonde one, who always loved playing with her guitar in choir practice. I finally went to choir, only because Mikey was there, and I always loved watching and listening to him sing. Jessica was always sitting reading a book, like literally every day! I don't know how much you can read a day, but she can read for IRELAND! Gloria was my new best friend. Naomi was the quiet one, who literally never speaks. Aoife was always obsessed with penguins, and always trying to steal Gloria away from me! She still is. Josephine, the drama queen, never stopped talking. And then there was Lucy.... Lucy was to be my first ever girlfriend. My first, and last.

Before I start talking about a GIRLFRIEND, back to the GIRL SQUAD!

As the days went on we all sat together during lunch and break, talking about weird book names like *Sisterhood of Travelling Pants* or something. I had no idea if it was a genuine group of friends, or a bloody book club!

We became so close and they made me feel so confident, get me, wearing my blazer over my legs rather than having it on me, for example. I was the only guy as well to be wearing a school jumper. It was a girl thing.

The only crap thing about being friends with girls was that I was never invited to the sleepovers because at the end of the day I still had a willy.

Everyday with the girls was amazing but having those strong butterfly feelings for Mikey was making me feel so weird I couldn't stop staring at him during the lunch and morning breaks. I did in fact have a really pretty distraction aside from this, not a distraction from my sexuality, but a distraction because I was genuinely distracted by Lucy's wonderful beauty. I will be talking about Lucy, AKA my ex girlfriend, in a bit but right now we have to talk about ELLA NEELY! The one and only!

It was a normal day in the classroom where I was casually sitting on my own waiting for the bell to ring so I could go see the squad in the canteen. Suddenly, this girl with long, brown, straight hair, with the most beautiful smile, sat beside me and started giggling.

To be honest I thought she was just going to take the piss out of me as the whole class were just staring at me waiting for something to happen but she genuinely needed to sit beside me because she fell out with her other friend and she didn't want to look like a loner so she literally just used me so she wouldn't look like a loner. Imagine. Cheers mate.

I had my *High School Musical* pencil case placed on the side of my desk along with my books and Ella, that was her name, was like "Oh My God I love Zac Efron". I whispered back, "Me too". To be fair I didn't know if I fancied her or if I was completely obsessed with her because it was so unusual for someone to choose to sit beside me and talk to me as well. By the looks of things her and her friend weren't going to be best buds again so it looked like I had my first friend during class times. I am pretty sure all the boys in my class were so jealous because she picked me to sit beside. They looked raging! And she was and still is a stunner.

Days turned into weeks, weeks turned into months and we swapped phone numbers and were constantly texting each other, calling each other's house phones, it was amazing!

I actually had something fun to tell when I got home from school. Has my life got a little better now that Ella and the girls are now in my life…?

Now that I've sealed a good friendship with not just the girls in the canteen but also with Ella Neely, the hottest girl in my class, I was hoping to figure out what this feeling was inside me. Do I fancy girls or did I fancy boys?

CHAPTER FOUR
Boys

I pretty much thought about Mikey everyday in the hallway while we walked past each other, it was so hard, I just wanted to stop and kiss him and tell him how much he meant to me but at the same time I didn't want my head kicked in, or even worse! DETENTION! Imagine detention feeling worse than a beating.

I am pretty sure everyone assumed I was gay, not that I ever said "Yes I am gay". That's the only thing I regret in school, I wish I had stood up for myself and said "NO, I am not gay!" I was only a kid. How was I meant to know if I was gay or not?

During the second year in school my feelings got stronger for Mikey. I remember constantly going to cry in the toilets and going back to class feeling magically okay. The thing was, I didn't have anyone to talk to about it. My mum didn't know, I certainly couldn't talk to my dad about these feelings because he would probably get mad so I just cried it off in the toilets mostly everyday. I hate kids who literally have everything handed to them and they still seem to get upset about something, that was literally me. If only I knew then how much my mum did for me back then, why was I crying in the toilets on my own? Of course she would have been okay with it.

The canteen squad and I started doing things out of school, like going for lunch, Belfast trips on the bus and, most importantly, my FIRST SLEEPOVER!

CHAPTER FIVE
Sleepovers

All the girls never really wanted to ask their parents if I could come to their sleepovers because they were odd and mostly afraid in case they got in trouble, ugh just because I had a willy, BUT Laura's Mum was a legend! She invited me to Laura's sleepover and I was over the moon! I remember Mum was so excited that I was going to my first sleepover. My mum called my friend Laura's dad, partly because she couldn't believe it, and partly because they were planning everything I needed to bring, imagine!

Oh the excitement in our house that night! Welly boots, "wellingtons", because she has a really big river in her garden, pjs, to sleep in, obvs, and most importantly, MYSELF!

Me, on a girlie sleepover. OMG.

The sleepover clan included Laura, Gloria, Jessica, Josephine, Aoife and the one and only Lucy.

It was around 11:30 at night, we were running around in Laura's big house, and Lucy and I were constantly staring each other out. It was weird because I never looked at Mikey like the way I looked at Lucy. I looked at Lucy like I wanted to keep her safe and warm and just wanted to give her a kiss.

Lucy was playing hard to get, I was clearly coming on to her. I was a different boy that night. My camp, gay side was away because there was this other side of me that I had no clue even existed. What were these feelings?

During that night we all decided to sleep in a row of six beside each other (as Laura had loads of room) and Lucy and I held hands under the covers. That was the start of it. Who knew what this was.

I started to pay more attention to Lucy more than normal during each day of the week in school. We would text as much as I would text Ella but Lucy would get more kisses on each text message. Does that mean something? After meeting Ella and Lucy around the same time I knew that the way I felt about Lucy was way different from how I felt about Ella. I liked Lucy a lot. I wanted to look out for her and I wanted to make her happy. Each day Mikey was slowly leaving my mind and Lucy was quickly rushing in.

It was near the end of the school year and I was having such a great time getting to know Lucy. She told her mum I was her gay best friend but we all know I was much more than that. We spent everyday together in school and mostly every night together as well, things were moving quite fast. My acceptance in Laura's house allowed me to be accepted in Lucy's. It was a wonderful feeling but was it because I was seen to be gay?

I was able to talk to Ella about all my feelings for Lucy during Math class and she told me just to go for it and don't hold back so one day I did it. I KISSED Lucy! It was the end of the school year before leaving and returning back as third years and we kissed in the school field, while the sun was shining and the birds were humming. I remember it so well. All the boys from my class were able to watch it as they were out playing football, of course without me, not like I wanted to play football anyway. This was much better!

Lucy became a part of my life very quickly. It was something that I was able to talk to my dad about, Lucy, which actually felt quite good. To have at last something in common to talk about, girls, and how you deal with them on a day to day basis. Lucy not only became a part of my life really quickly but she was also invited to almost every family event and was able to sleepover. Of course we would have to sleep in different beds but when my parents fell asleep I was able to sneak out of my sister's old room at the time, because she was away travelling abroad, and I snuck into my room where Lucy was always sleeping. Sleeping means she was waiting up for me to come in so we could have a little session of kissing and cuddles and what not, wink wink!

I was really enjoying summer break with Lucy, then we came back to school during third year and it was unbelievably different. Everyone stopped picking on me because I was now with a girl. How they knew that was because there were loads of pictures of us together on my *Bebo* profile. I was so proud and looking forward to being accepted for once. Social media then worked wonders for me.

God I miss *Bebo*.

CHAPTER SIX
Drama drama

I was in my third year and life was good. I actually started to play football with the boys during break, well tried to, haha.

My friendships with the girls got stronger. I started getting to know Aoife, aka one of the members of the canteen squad, a lot more! She was the one who was literally always obsessed with penguins. She was always so skinny it made me jealous because I was slowly putting the weight on and off and I just wanted my weight to stay as one weight and look good but of course my life wasn't about staying at one place. It never was.

During the third year in school, I was attending a theatre group up in Lisburn which is like 40 mins away from my hometown. I would have been in numerous shows with them where I performed and sung on stage along with the other members of the group, who I liked to call friends as well. Of course things weren't straight forward as I fell for one of the members of the group, Stephen. The tall, dark and handsome guy you always would picture in a children's book or a sexy movie. A dream guy no matter what.

Things were still going well with Lucy and I. She would come and see me perform, watching me at my best but behind the scenes was just a disaster.

Here we go again.

Sharing a dressing room with a guy who you literally think you are falling for isn't really good for the mind and soul and I slowly started to crumble during the next 4 years in theatre.

We were travelling everywhere, Buxton in England, Waterford and even London! Things started to get heated with Lucy and I as we were getting older and we started experimenting more in the bedroom. I enjoyed it and so did she. Nothing was really wrong with us until I started that theatre group. I was so busy and my feelings between Lucy and Stephen, never mind Mikey who was just about to leave the school for good, as it was his last year, meant my head was everywhere.

Not that things weren't hard enough between Lucy and I, the theatre group I was in was offered to go on TV to do a stint on the show *Don't Stop Believing* with *Channel 5*. I had to choose between my relationship with Lucy and flying over to England for a family wedding or fly to London to perform on TV.

My heart was with the performing. Even though it had its ups and downs I belonged.

After weeks of fighting with Lucy, because she didn't want me to go, I decided to let her down and take the offer to go on *Channel 5*. I didn't think it was the right decision at the time to go with her. I had to follow my heart, as much as I loved her it just wasn't meant to be at such a young age. She will always be my first love and I will always remember how I felt around her. Straight or gay... I still loved her and that was the most important thing.

That was the end of the relationship I once had with her. I felt heartbroken. I remember crying so hard leaning on my mums knees. I couldn't eat for weeks. I needed my energy for performing but I just couldn't eat. What was wrong with me? I thought, is this what it's like to be actually heart broken? I know I was only like 15 years old but I had seen her everyday in school and everyday after school. I thought my world was falling apart.

CHAPTER SEVEN
Showtime

I got the opportunity to pack and leave for a week to go to London at the age of 15. That was probably one of the hardest things I ever had to do on my own without having my mum there to tell me everything was going to be okay. I had to keep my head high and stay strong because after all i was going into a competition which was airing on TV!

It was such a long week. I was travelling everywhere, mostly on buses, they always make me horny. We covered loads of video shoots, went to the recording studio and pre recorded our song for the live shows. We would learn our dance, try and eat healthily and yet try and still have a good time. Everyone in the group was so used to being away from home but I really wasn't. Yes, it was great living the dream but I had no one really to share it with. I didn't have a group of friends.Yes, I would have fun with certain ones but I was never invited to join them for lunch or anything. I had to make my own way around sometimes and deal with it. Which was okay because I was used to that when I was growing in primary school but I thought all that was behind me.

The day of the live show was amazing. Walking out on stage in front of thousands of people and of course millions on TV, was amazing. The lights on my shoulders and the feel of the soft stage floor. It was life changing. I knew from then on that I wanted to be a star every day on stage. It was just a shame I never had the confidence to do it solo.

My family at home were able to watch me, esp Granda. He really enjoyed it! He was so proud of the promotional posters framed and hung up on the house. It's still there.

I actually hated flying. I always think planes are going to crash like literally every time I get on one. It was horrible. It never gets easier, well that's what I thought back in the day but now I get a flight at least seven times a year, depending on what show I am filming, but we will get to that part later!

It was during the summer when I performed on *Channel 5* so I got to thinking about how I was going to work things out with Lucy before school restarted or would I just leave it.

That was a long summer.

I was able to do another show with the theatre group and my feelings for Stephen became much stronger than normal and I was at breaking point were I just had to say something to him. "Stephen… I really like you". I wrote to him on facebook as it was the new thing back then and everyone was literally using it.

His response was not good. Despite the rumours of him being bisexual he did not take it well when I told him how I felt and he responded so aggressively and horrible. I will never forget it. Of course I was sad but why should I feel like a victim again? First not being able to say anything to Mikey about how I felt, then for me to finally open up about my feelings to Stephen only for him to throw them back in my face. I was devastated but also angry! Where did that emotion come from? This was new for me.

made a promise to myself that from now on if I fancy someone I will not fight the fear and go for it, I will stay quiet. Is this why I'm alone now? Whether it be a boy or a girl, in the past, from then on it has always been for boys. I think I was slowly turning into my normal self. The real me, perhaps.

CHAPTER EIGHT
Revelations and celebrations

It was a couple of days before school started back and I just had to tell my mum how I felt about life in general and about how I was meant to deal with liking boys.

Every gay kid has this fear of "coming out" to their parents. I don't think I ever came out because people always assumed I was always gay, and at such a young age, so I think If I didn't have that happen to me then, when I was younger, maybe growing up would have been easier.

I walked down the creaky stairs, so straight away my mum knew I was coming down to talk to her. She was sitting in the kitchen finishing her amazing pasta, that she literally makes every week of her life. I sat down and said "I think we need to talk about something". Despite knowing herself what I was going to say, because it was blatantly obvious that I was always on the edge of the gay train, she stopped eating. My heart was literally going to fall out of my ass! I was so nervous and scared! I had that funny lying face I have when I'm telling a little fib or confessing to something I shouldn't be saying (same as my sister). "Mum, I think, well I know, I kinda like boys". As soon as I said it I quickly put my head down and begged for the table to swallow me up and hide me! It was pure silence for at least 3 seconds. It felt like the longest 3 seconds of my entire life!

"First of all, I will love you no matter who you are" she said. YES! Those words, I will love you! They made my heart beat even more but in a good way. She was okay with it. She explained to me that I should talk to my dad and that I shouldn't call myself gay until I know for certain if I like it or not!

If you ever thought my mum would be awkward, when I told my sister she brought up words I didn't even know existed, safe sex, condoms, lube, sexually transmitted diseases, AIDS, HIV, the whole lot! She was just making sure I would stay safe because she knows how easy it is to put yourself at risk. She has been a student and has seen lots. She was always there for me when I needed her and now I could talk to her about stuff like that. How lucky was I?

Not that I had done anything at that age anyway, well not yet. MWAHAHA!

School started back and I was now in Fourth year!

Time flies when you're having fun! I woke up in the early hours of the morning because I was determined to look good for the first day of school. Mikey was finally gone, Lucy was apparently with someone else, she was keen and I was living the first day of my real life! I woke up, got my breakfast handed to me as per usual by Mum, I remember exactly what I had for breakfast that morning, garlic toast, with pasta sauce! I know, quite weird for a breakfast but as I have learned I was quite a weird young boy! This was also the first year where we can all skip the canteen and go downtown and go for a chippy during lunch hours, woohoo!

The long fringe was straightened, using my mums straighteners. My mascara was on fleek, yes for the first time I tried mascara on, and I looked amazing! I put some lip gloss on and I walked out the door with my head held high. I, Ronan Rice, will not let anyone bully me this year, I will not take no for an answer and I will pass all my exams, well most of them anyway!

I got the bus wearing my blazer on my knees for everyone to see and talk about. I was so obsessed with Mikey I didn't really notice how hot the guys actually were in my class! OMG Tom, hello!!!

I sat beside Gloria on the bus, she loved my new look. She thought I looked really good, which was amazing to hear as I had just fixed my hair up, that's really all, but hey I look really good! The confidence was oozing.

It was the first day of class and it was amazing. I sat beside Ella, we were planning to have a sleepover the following night, that we couldn't wait for, so we just had to do it on that night! We went to school the following day together it was so much fun! Things were looking up.

CHAPTER NINE
It's Britney, Bitch

When news got out that the only gay boy in school finally came out everyone went crazy. Of course I heard the same phrases, "you dropped your gay card", "you are a faggot", "you are this and that" but I couldn't be bothered listening so I just smiled and walked on and pretended I was Britney Spears.

Why hadn't I ever noticed how beautiful Tom is! He was also a dark haired guy with lovely eyes and a beautiful smile. He was the cutest guy in the class. I had to sit beside him during french class which was literally amazing because I got to be around him and actually talk to him and copy his homework and just being able to be in that love bubble was amazing.

Of course he was always straight but there was always something about him that was so gentle and trusting. I really wanted to tell him how I felt but we all know what happens when Ronan tells the truth! So I didn't say anything, well not for a while yet. I kept it super quiet and only told Ella. I didn't want him to move seats then I would have had to sit beside someone else.

Every lunchtime I would sit on top of the wall with the canteen squad and watch Tom play football. He was so fast on the pitch and so hot. I kept shouting "Take your top off" then I had to duck down and pretend it was Saoirse who was shouting it. I really enjoyed living in that love bubble again. I just wanted everything to fall into place. I even went on Google and looked up love spells to try and get him to fall in love with me and of course they didn't work. Piece of shit. We would text each other during the weekends but not flirty texting. Like boy texting, about girl problems he had or advice on girls. As part of the canteen girl squad I was always there for him with my inside knowledge but was he never there for me...

CHAPTER TEN
Home

I got home that day thinking, "Okay. I think I can deal with this. It's not that hard to be gay in school." I was having such a great time mingling with different groups of girls and being able to talk to literally like three guys without being hit or offended. Life was good.

I got upstairs to get dressed after going to my Nanny Dee's, which I always love because she makes great food and gives me the biggest plate. I always knew I was her favourite and of course I still am! She is alive and kicking (and also farting very much everyday if you check my Snapchat daily). So I went upstairs to get my uniform off and my dad kept screaming at my mum so she started to get a bit louder back at him. I walked downstairs and they went quiet. I haven't heard them argue in a while. Was I too selfish with my own problems that I wasn't looking out for my mum?

I was right... they did have problems. My dad had done the dirtiest and most disgusting thing, he cheated on my mum and had been for a while. Cold heartedly cheated on my mum. Why would you even? She is so hard working, puts everyone first and so pretty!

I don't really want to get into it. There is no point in dwelling on this as it is done. I'm not going to waste my time on it. It was yet another hard year for myself but more importantly for my mum. He let us all down, he wasn't just letting my mum down but he was letting me down too. Being a father figure is so important but that day he ruined it. He broke my family's heart and left us to pick up the pieces. I just thought "what an idiot". There is no way I am bonding with you now after that.

Mum was a little bit broken for a while and I hated seeing her so upset. I didn't really know what to do with the anger or feelings I had towards my dad so I let it out like any young boy would do!

I went on *YOUTUBE!*

Yes the good old *YouTube* that would literally change my life forever.

CHAPTER ELEVEN
Fame

I remember everything about it. I remember what I was wearing on the night I recorded the video and what song I used. I made a little short music video of me dancing in the kitchen and it got almost 500 views in a hour. Back then that was really good because I had no idea what was good or bad and the fact that 500 people had viewed this was just amazing. Social media wasn't that big back then so when you got at least 500 views you knew things were looking up for you!

Of course I showed my mum and she loved it, and I thought no one I actually knew would see the video, because after all, I hadn't that many friends to share it with.

That night sleeping was probably one of the last sleeps I had being an normal average boy as I knew it.

Waking up was weird, I didn't think anything of the video I posted on YouTube. It was just a normal day but I had a weird feeling. I went to school and straight away people on the bus were just staring me out. Did I have something on my face? Were people whispering about me? What the hell was going on?

I texted Ella while I was on the bus and said "Why is everyone talking about me?" She quickly texted back saying "your video!!"

I walked into school with everyone just laughing at me, copying the dance moves. Some people were like "oh my

Ronan. Your video was literally so good, make more!". I even had people saying hi to me that would never say hi to me before. I went into our class and it felt like I was walking down the aisle at a wedding, all eyes were on you and only you! I sat beside Ella and said "Everyone has seen that video". Ella went on her crappy phone (well it was actually a blackberry so it was quite good back in the day). She searched my video and guess how many views I had?

1,700 in the space of 24 hours! What was going on?!

I couldn't believe people were actually talking about me. Did I like it?

The canteen squad and my ex girlfriend, were so shocked to have seen the video and how much of an impact it had on the school in just one day. During that day I went into the toilets and just stared at myself in the mirror, is this what I really want? Do I want to be a normal school boy with good grades or do I want to be something extraordinary?

Days went on and I thought about making another video but this time a meaningful one. My Granda was sadly going through the stages of cancer and I thought about making a nice video about him. It wasn't a dance video but a nice video with a beautiful song. I made it just for him. Not many people knew what the video was about, especially my family, but now they do. It didn't get many views but I knew in my heart that it was a success. And it came from my heart.

As life went on in fourth year my video star fame started to increase where if I went to the cinema with my mum someone would always have something to say.

Was I an internet sensation? Or a fool.

I sit here and write this questioning myself about was I or wasn't I. I never really had the time to sit down and think about all of things I did in the past and I am actually quite proud of starting my own *YouTube* Channel because I don't think I would have the confidence I have today if it wasn't for the videos being such a success.

CHAPTER TWELVE
Loss

My Granda sadly passed away during October, the month of my birthday. It was very sad and the family was broken but we were such a strong family we all stuck together and I found I had amazing friends.

All the girls came to the funeral, it was so nice of them to come and meant a lot to me. I lost a bit of myself for a while but I knew that he would never have wanted me to lose who I was as a person and I wanted to be there for Nanny. Even my dad was there for Mummy while they were going through that rough patch. That was something he actually done right, maybe too late, but probably the only thing he has ever done right in my eyes.

The school year got harder after the funeral. I couldn't focus on grades because I was once again getting bullied because I officially came out and probably because of the videos.

There are so many things your friends can say and do to help you out, but you really are on your own if you are getting bullied in school. Being bullied makes you do silly things, as we all know, but what it made me do in the end was rebel.

I was always such a nice kid, didn't smoke, didn't do drugs didn't even drink but when I turned sixteen and in my final year of school I was a mess.

I wasn't taking drugs or smoking but I was binge drinking on the streets with my so called friends. I was also sneaking into bars and drinking with people I shouldn't have been drinking with but in school I was still being bullied. Just being able to do my own thing outside of school helped me relax a bit. Things came really crashing down when Dan entered my life.

"Daniel", every time I say his name in my head I actually just want to cry. He made my last year of school a nightmare. Dan was also a dark haired guy with a nice body, large group of friends and a typical high school lad who had the girlfriend, played sports and drove a pretty car after he left school. He was a couple of years above me when he left school and he went on to go to college. This meant he got to learn how to drive, passed his driving test and became more independent so of course he would want things that nobody else needed to know about but messaging me was one of the biggest regrets of his life.

CHAPTER THIRTEEN
Possibilities

My social media following was getting bigger each day and with each new video being uploaded more people were finding out that I was the only gay in school or, as you say, in the "village". I got a random message from Dan saying "Would you like to meet up? Maybe sometime after school or before?"

I 100 percent thought this is definitely someone taking the piss out of me. Or maybe he was going to meet up with me and probably beat me up, I didn't tell anyone, only Ella and Gloria. I thought about it and thought about it and then I was like, why not meet him? Maybe he could be the one. Should I miss out on this opportunity? When has anybody asked me out or even be remotely interested in me after Lucy broke up with me? This was also a guy! I had never been with a guy before like, ever, and this could be the first time I get to try out 'stuff' with a guy and possibly really enjoy it! After all I am sixteen, I thought.

Wednesday morning came and I agreed to meet him during my first Religious Studies class. I picked that day because I loved Mrs Bell and I never missed a class and I thought she would most likely let me get away with missing one class. Sorry Mrs Bell! I was going to pretend I was at the dentist or something. I got to the bus station feeling all nervous, telling Saoirse to get on the bus and don't tell anyone where I was off too and I'll text her when I am on my way back to school. She was really nervous for me as she didn't think it was a good idea at all but I was so in over my head that day that I didn't really know what I was actually thinking but I did it anyway. I went along the bus station at the back and he picked me up and we drove away.

Getting into his car, was weird. The smell of his aftershave turned me on straight away. I knew this wasn't going to be a chit chat kinda meet. I knew what was going to happen. It was too late to say no, he was already driving.

I thought I felt special that he picked me to be in his car, but the way he pushed my head down to hide me from the other ones waiting for the bus was a wake up call for me to get out of the car, but when does Ronan Rice ever do anything stupid or outrageous? I was a completely different person that day, feeling brave and in control, or maybe that's the person I was meant to be.

We drove down to the famous Inch Abbey. It's all dark and gloomy under the bridge and straight away he kissed me. My first kiss. This kiss, with a guy, was so passionate and even though it was in a car (not ideal) it was still so magical. Everything I had been through was nothing compared to this kiss. The way he held me in his car, every drop of feeling, from his fingers on my side to his lips touching my neck for the first time, ooohhh it was a feeling I will never forget. I knew I liked him.

The feeling of knowing finally someone wants me, someone likes me was just too much. I didn't have sexy boxers on that day. I remember he laughed when he took my trousers off because I had chips and burger emoji's on my boxers and he thought they were quite cool! The windows started to steam up, the sound of kisses was crystal clear and the quiet music on his radio in the background was all so romantic. This was bliss.

Don't worry, I didn't have sex with him in his car, but we pretty much did everything else except sex! I was okay with that. I wasn't ready to have sex. He drove back to school and stopped the car half way down the street, he kissed me and said "I'll see you again". I was so excited to see him again.

When I walked into class straight away Mrs Bell looked at me and said "so tell me… who was he?" Ella had already told Mrs Bell where I was! Thanks Ella. She was okay with it but told me off for skipping class and told me not to do it again. I loved being able to go home after a hard day at school and being able to text someone who really enjoys talking to me and who wanted every bit of my body and more. I loved that feeling.

I wanted to be his and only his but after finding out something that would literally make me feel sick, it ruined it all. HE HAD A GIRLFRIEND! Yes, a girlfriend. He cheated on his girlfriend. I did not know that he was even seeing someone and then after Ella telling me he was seeing someone who was pretty with dark, long hair made me feel sick to the stomach that I was a part of something so bad. My dad did this type of thing, not me.

I was so angry and upset that he used me and I felt like I was in the wrong.

I opened up and told the wrong person at the wrong time and the whole school found out about what we both were getting up to. It was so awful because no one ever believed me and people took his side over mine. I was left out in the cold, again, while he could go back to his perfect life and perfect girlfriend to leave me to pick up his mess.

People questioned me, people who grew up in school with me, certain girls thought I was lying. Why would I lie about something like that? Why would I lie at all? The following week was horrible. I don't think I have ever been so unhappy. I walked into school after begging my Mum to let me stay off, walking down that long hallway, everyone staring at you, laughing at you, pushing me. Life was not good.

The only teacher that ever looked out for me was Mrs Bell. It was disgusting how the school handled things, especially bullying. I felt alone. I also felt a bit broken hearted as I grew to have strong feelings for Dan. I felt like I had got dumped. I had to start walking up home because people always abused me on the bus for "lying" about their so called friend. I was so annoyed as none of my friends had my back, only the canteen squad and Ella. I'll remember that guys!

That was the start of my boy issues that I still have to this day, which is quite sad because I think I could have had a healthy relationship if it wasn't for so many guys screwing me over when they had the chance to. I fall for people way too easily and always get hurt. That will be one important thing I'll tell my kids one day, don't be a pushover when it comes to men, or women. I want to teach them that you are beautiful, and you are nobody's second best. You are first and always will be first.

Screw you Dan.

CHAPTER FOURTEEN
Rollercoaster

Its safe to stay that school was a roller coaster.

Being bullied everyday for five years, being in a relationship with a girl then moving on from that to being used by complete knob heads, along with horrible family problems, I was glad to see school finishing. I will miss all my girls but I know I will stay friends with them for life. I mean for LIFE.

As the weeks started to roll on and we were into having only days left I was finally able to enjoy it. I was so emotional. I loved my friends, they were there for me through thick and thin and never will I forget that, I was so sad that Ella and I would no longer be sitting together every day. I was thinking in my head.... Will I ever see Ella again? Will I be able to see her everyday when school finishes? I will miss such small moments like watching Ella sharpen her pencils so perfectly and having them in the correct order. I will miss the giggles during math class. I would also miss how happy I feel when I see Ella walk into the classroom towards me to sit down. I will miss the canteen squad and the amazing CURRY!

I don't think I would have got through school if it wasn't for my amazing family, my mum and my friends! Crossgar, it has been a blast and a hell of a nightmare. Peace out!

CHAPTER FIFTEEN
Journeys

I applied for a course up in Lisburn College for acting. I got a letter of acceptance a couple of weeks after I finished school. Sadly mum and I had to move out of the family home a couple of months after finishing school, so goodbye Downpatrick and hello Belfast!

Moving to Belfast was a big step as my family were in Downpatrick. I was super nervous but yet so excited to have a brand new start up in the big city! I heard that the food up there is pretty amazing. I couldn't bloody wait.

I had such a great start at Lisburn College. I was so confident and had a really good relationship with the tutor's and my classmates. I made some amazing friends, friends I thought I would have for life. My tutors were so cool. I loved Jenny and Sarah as they really taught me so much that I still remember today. Treat people the way you want to be treated and be kind to others, and also do your bloody work on time, haha. I had different kinds of friends in college. I had the band geeks, who were actually quite cool to be around. I had my friends in class, mostly girls. My girls, I love them. I had some friends outside of class, I was loving life. Sleepovers every weekend, messy nights out and dinner nights in. What more could you ask for?

It was quite annoying living in Belfast because Mummy still worked in Downpatrick so I didn't get to see her during the day or in the morning. I had to learn to get the buses on my own which was a big step for me. I was alone a lot though.

I still travelled to my theatre group but I started taking panic attacks and this put a strain on my mum and I. She had to be called many times to come and help me out and this put a strain on her.

I was diagnosed with ADHD since I was a youngster and I took medication for it every morning, hence why I got so drunk, because I shouldn't even be drinking with my meds (but I do it anyway because it gives me a buzz). I got the bus everyday to college and got used to it eventually. It wasn't fun but at least I wasn't bullied on it.

There was always this guy back home in Downpatrick who I always had a thing for and to be honest we did meet up during the school year but it was kind of a secret. I didn't really mention it to you guys because I didn't even want him in my book but since I am telling you all the truth it was Justin Yes, Justin from *One Night With My Ex.* We fell in love at such a young age, after I left school. I kept it very secret and we had some sleepovers and late night walks. My mum got to meet him and I thought he was a keeper. He was that one guy who made me feel perfect, beautiful and content. I was so in love with him! I would do anything for him, he was my rock and I was his.

Do you know when you hold hands in the playground and you get that butterfly feeling in your stomach? Well that's what I get when I see Justin.

Things were going really well for once between the both of us then all the rumours started circulating that he was cheating on me. There are always so many rumours about me since I started making videos on YouTube, people just really like to talk utter bullshit and people actually believe it.

Justin and I were on and off for a good few years. When we were together and things were good we got on great. We broke up for good when I was in my second year of college and that was the last time we ever saw each other. I don't really want to talk about the good times and bad times with him because it was hard and this book is not about him. I don't think he deserves the time… soz.

During my second year of college I started putting a bit of weight on but still looked and felt good and it didn't stop me from having a good time. I don't think I ever laughed so much in my entire life, It was so good to have that laugh in college then come home to see the girls at home and even have more fun! I finally went on a dating app on my new phone that my mum bought me, Thanks MUM!

I took a smashing photo of myself and put it online and instantly got a message from this cute boy, "Hey Ronan, can I be in one of your videos?" Ugh NO! I am trying to find love, not a fan!

It's so hard actually trying to find someone who is genuinely interested in me since going on YouTube and now being on TV, but we will get to being on TV later. Let's talk more about me on this sexy dating app.

I was looking through my messages and this handsome man once again with dark hair - what is with me in guys with dark hair? He messaged me straight away saying "hey fancy a coffee?" So forward, I loved it. I didn't even like coffee but I replied "Yes of course, I love coffee" A little white lie won't hurt a fly. I had so much support from all my friends in college and back home aka Ella, Gloria and Aoife, sadly that was all I had left. The canteen squad went their separate ways. I still get to see Laura once or twice a year, which is great because I've always liked her! Aoife, Gloria and I stayed close. We are going to be friends for life!

I can't believe I am actually going on a date again! I haven't been on a date since Justin and I were together. I was still living in Belfast at the time so it wasn't that hard to travel, all I had to do was get ready and walk to the coffee place. What was it called... *Costa* or something? Oooh I couldn't think.

I was literally so nervous. My mum give me a big pep talk about how strong I am but I literally felt weak at the knees. I just wanted to walk back home, walking towards the place where he was meant to be standing at was killing me! I was so nervous what happens if he doesn't like me...? What happens if I don't like him? Oh my God, I need to fart! Should I fart now before I walk up to him? Screw this,I just did and it actually stinks!

The moment had arrived, I saw him, he was standing there so elegantly with a nice shirt and trousers, looked like he was going to work to be honest but I liked the look. It made me feel a bit excited down stairs, if you know what I mean? Wink Wink!

"Hi, are you Freddy?" I mumbled. "Yes, you look really nice Ronan" he said.

Oh my Lord, the way he said my name, I literally just wanted to jump on him and kiss him everywhere and I mean everywhere! He was so sweet and thoughtful. The night went on after ordering one tea and one coffee. Yes, I had to tell him I lied on my dating app profile, I hated coffee. As the night went on we slowly knew that something was going to progress. I just had a feeling guys.

As the days went on we had more dates. It was beautiful. He got to meet my mum plenty of times after she invited him to see a musical with us one night. We held hands, it was so romantic, I didn't even care who was looking. I wanted people to know that I was his and he was mine. I can't believe I was that happy. Was it all too good to be true, was he really a nice guy…?

CHAPTER SIXTEEN
Love

It was nearly a year and we still hadn't done it. I was so nervous but the good thing was he wasn't even that keen. He didn't put any pressure on me so why not wait until it was a magical night? I just didn't want to do it because I had to. I wanted to wait until it was special. There was one night where he finally got to sleepover at my house. I was really excited because I knew this was it! The night I finally could tell all my friends I finally had SEX!

I was so nervous. I knew all the do's and don'ts because my sister warned me. She is a legend! Mum was downstairs watching a really good movie, I was a bit sad because I really wanted to watch it but I had better things to be doing, oi oi!

Freddy and I went out that night for a nice bite to eat. We had a really good night and I just knew I wanted to do it. I took him back to mine and we watched Love Actually, pretty sure on repeat, but it was the best movie ever. We were both sitting on top of the bed because my room was so warm, Mum forgot to turn the heating off and it was nearly summer.

I remember exactly what time it was because Ella texted me saying "Well... did you do it?" It was 11:30 pm... it was time!

I was having weird flashbacks of all the boys that used me and messed with my head but I knew Freddy was never like that, I let him touch me knowing he felt the same. I loved him, his lips kissing my lips felt like the first kiss all over again, the soft feel of his shaved cheeks against my face while he kissed me. I remember stopping and I just looked at him and said, "Thank you" he said "for what" I said… "For loving me"

It wasn't painful. It wasn't sore, well after five minutes it started to feel AMAZING, It felt just right and I knew I was going to be with him forever. Also, thank God mum didn't hear anything because that would have been quite awkward.

I really enjoyed having a boyfriend that really loved me. I enjoyed my education and I enjoyed being independent. I could tell my mum noticed a change in me. It felt so good to know she was proud of me.

It was a couple of months after we first slept together and I was invited to my friends 18th party in a beautiful restaurant in Belfast. I really wanted to bring Freddy so he could finally meet the rest of my friends and I also wanted to see him (so I could see his big willy again).

My friends were all so excited to meet him but during the day I was getting really bad vibes from him. He wasn't responding to any of my messages, and when he was talking to me on the phone he just sounded really off. I just prayed to God I didn't say anything that had upset him. I don't think I did? I was with my friends that day and we were going to meet Freddy at the designated place. It was around 6:30 pm and we were all walking up to the place and there he was, with a guy, and looked really edgy and caught out.

I was so confused because I never even knew he was meeting up with a friend that day at all. I said hi and kissed him and straight away I tasted whiskey. He was never that big of a drinker so straight away I knew something was wrong. I just didn't understand why he didn't say anything about his plans that day. I was a bit confused. He didn't even introduce me to his friend. His friend just said talk to you later Freddy and walked off, what the hell! How embarrassing was this and how did I look in front of all my friends? Straight away my friends judged him and that was the one thing I didn't want to happen. I hate that!

We were all at the dinner table, it was buffet. Yes, I buffet! I love constant food! I was so excited to have the salted chilli chicken, that is literally my favourite food ever, I got like two plates of it and wanted to go up for thirds and then I got up and straight away he looked at me and said, "Don't you think you've had enough?" I just paused and sat back down again not even knowing everyone else was listening to our conversation. I just sat there staring at a stranger. Where was the Freddy I gave my virginity too, fair enough I was eating too much, probably, but the tone of his voice and his manner was completely off. I felt ashamed of myself that night.

I really was looking forward to the cake, I never got it.

As the relationship went on it got worse. He would constantly shout at me for silly things such as, not holding his hand in public, not kissing him back when we were on the bus. He just turned into this horrible guy, not the guy I once loved. It was then I heard several rumours from a friend that he goes out to clubs and cheats on me like literally every weekend. I was so hurt and I knew straight away it was true. His attitude changed straight after we had sex. Was I not good enough for him, was I not skinny or beautiful…?

I confronted him one night when he came to my house with LOVE BITES literally all over his neck. What the hell! Literally came into my house with bites on his neck so casual saying ah it was just a friend messing around. I am sorry but do I give Ella love bites when I get bored... NO! "Get out of my house, literally I want you to leave, don't ever speak to me again". I felt so stupid to let myself fall for yet another knob.

Why was finding true love so hard? During my emotional break up my mum and I decided to move back to Downpatrick to be closer to the family. I was happy because I really needed my family's support at the moment. Mum found it difficult supporting me when she was in Downpatrick so often while running up and down to Belfast.

Aoife started to get pretty busy with school and starting University. I had hardly even seen Gloria at all and I would see Ella like once every couple of weeks. Was I losing myself in the middle of this relationship disaster aftermath?

CHAPTER SEVENTEEN
Home comforts

Living back home was great. I started going out of my comfort zone, meeting old friends and making new ones. The more videos I made the more people knew who I was. It was great having people being nice to me. I started drinking most weekends, well every weekend. Every video I made the more I got noticed on nights out.

Nights out were meant to be fun but they literally turned into meet and greets and all I wanted to do was just have fun and let my hair down without having to listen to people's thoughts and opinions. The only thing that kept me from being paranoid was just to get wasted! Oh alcohol tasted so good when you earned the money to buy it. I was working in town during that stage so I was able to buy my own drink instead of asking Mum all the time. I was spending so much money on just drink, it was so bad!

Ella hated going out with me when I was drinking because I always got too drunk for her and we always fell out so I made a group of friends that I would like to call the drinking buddies. I loved them. The good thing was that I could see them during the day and do cool things together and then drink at night. I loved it!

As each month went on my personality was changing. I was going home every night with a different guy, I stopped making videos, which was one of the things I was passionate about. I showed up to work several times drunk and I didn't even care. I was a mess, I even let my ex boyfriend Justin back into my life during one very drunken weekend.

My mum and I were having major problems due to my drinking because I really shouldn't be drinking with the meds. Remember I have ADHD! Mum tried to support me as much as she could but I didn't want to know.

It was around the time when College was finishing and I had nothing to do so I started drinking during the day until my whole world came crashing down one stupid night. I decided to take my medication a couple of hours before my drinking session started. I just really liked the buzz I got when I took them with drink.

It was a crazy night, all throughout the night I was getting really weird pains in my chest and I couldn't speak right. I wasn't enjoying the buzz or the night out. I kept bumping into things, making a mess out of everything. My mum was away to America so I had a couple of friends from work around that night. We got back and we had more drinks. I don't remember much of what happened only what people have told me. I drunk way too much and passed out on my bedroom floor and apparently stopped breathing, but before I passed out I had called the police but couldn't speak as I was so out of it.

I woke up to policemen in my mum's house, and my friends downstairs giving off. It was horrible, how one stupid, silly mistake can make things a whole lot worse. Of course the next morning I called Mum. I was confused about what had happened and didn't know if I wanted to go on with this habit or lifestyle. I wanted to change my ways and sort out my life before worse things could happen! Whenever Mum came back home from America we had a serious talk about how we can change my ways and how to move forward. We made a couple of calls and appointments with the doctor's regarding my ADHD and drinking. I was signed up to a six week program in Belfast to help me with alcohol and drug abuse. Not many people knew about this only Ella and my mum. I kept it very quiet and didn't talk to anyone about it! It sounds so serious when you say alcohol and drug abuse but it was serious. I could have died. The doctor said the buzz I get from drinking with my medication is the equivalent of taking cocaine.

Time to stop.

I didn't like the program. I wanted to leave each time I went in. I hated going through the pain and the experience and I never wanted to talk to anyone about it until now. I think the reason why I have written about it on here is maybe to bring awareness to others that there is help for people out there for those with drinking problems.

After those six weeks finally finished, I felt much better, fresh and alive. I wanted to do fun things that didn't involve drinking but I never had anyone to do that with as all my 'friends' were drinkers. I even went out on nights out and didn't drink. I sat there beside a table with everyone drinking shots, wine, beer, everything! I was drinking water or coke most nights. I still wanted to go out because the only way I could see my friends was if I went out and was sociable. Maybe I needed new friends that weren't into the party scene but I couldn't afford to lose any more friends.

CHAPTER EIGHTEEN
Happy New Year

It was a new year, new me, as they say. I was very excited for the year ahead. I was so excited because I was planning to make a little comeback on YouTube. It had been months and I hadn't made any more videos and I kind of missed the feeling of making one. I got a really good green screen from Santa the year before (although I didn't appreciate it then! What was that all about, Santa?!) and I was able to make amazing music videos.

I was planning to go to university, something I never thought was going to happen. All my classmates had applied the year before me but I wasn't ready then. I was so negative towards the fact that I just knew I wasn't going to get in. I applied for at least 5 universities and each month I was getting back bad news. By the end of it I didn't get into any of them . There was an option on the website were I could apply for one more university. I really didn't know what to do so I did the obvious thing anyone else would do... LETS GO AND SEE A MEDIUM!

I did so much research, I wanted to get the best person to "read my future". I had always believed in everything, such as the Easter Bunny, Santa, the Tooth Fairy and even mermaids. I swear I had seen one in Ballyhornan beach one day!

I completed my research and I planned to bring my bestie Ella with me. I had to. I couldn't do it on my own and my mum really wasn't interested in the idea of it. I got her address and number and Ella got the sat nav out and there we went. We were on our way to find out our destiny! I needed to find out what God had in plan for me. I was so lost and I didn't want to apply for another place in university if I wasn't going to get in.

We finally got to her house after making so many wrong turns. We walked out of the car and straight away got good vibes! She was so cool looking and had a real edgy look. I loved it. Her house was so cool and really warm! I was freezing that day so It was good to have a nice fire to warm me up. She offered me a drink, a cigarette or some food. I had to say yes for a wee drink, I was quite thirsty. "Ronan could I get you to go first?" she asked. I was so happy! I was like ''YES!'' I left Ella on her own in this stranger's house. Sorry Ella, tough luck, mucker.

We got into her little room, again it was very warm and edgy with a nice candle lit glowing in a room with comfy chairs. We sat down and straight away she wanted to let me know that I don't need to keep saying sorry to people. She made me pick out some cards, Success, Love and Health. I had no idea what these cards were.

I swear on my life, as soon as I sat on the chair I felt someone's hand on my shoulders. She looked up and said ''we have someone with you today Ronan''. I was worried because I had no idea who was touching me and it was all suddenly so cold in such a warm house. She said he is claiming to be an old gentleman, a daddy figure… I cried straight away. It was my cute Granda. I was over the moon, I wasn't expecting to have him here with me today. He was able to tell her things she could never have known, like what I whispered to him when he was in the coffin, during the wake, "Sorry that I can't hold your hand". I had said that. How

AMAZING was that? She knew what I had said. Not even my family knew what I whispered that day, never mind a stranger. I got a lot of information that day, I was going to move to a house near a beach, I was going to fly over the seas to study!! She saw me in flashing lights! I was getting so much from her I loved it then the one thing that I remember. "Ronan you will have a reunion with one of your past lovers." The name, John, or Justin. I was like "yes, Justin!" I had no idea what she meant as I would never go back with Justin, like ever, but little did I know I would be on a TV show with him in years to come!

Ella liked her reading as well! We both had a really good day! As soon as I got home I applied for Swansea University. I just had a feeling it was Swansea! I was so positive and knew I was going to get in!

CHAPTER NINETEEN
Goodbyes

For those few months I was taking life really easy, working in Downpatrick still and sleeping over at my Nanny Dee's house, mostly every weekend. God I love sleepovers with Nanny Dee. We would normally watch a class movie with some pizza and then some sweets after… she really is the best. I was spending more time with my aunty and her adorable kids. However I was a bit sad because If I was going to study overseas how will I be able to spend time with the kids twice a week?

Family is so important to me. I think If I ever did turn into a "Star" I would never change when it comes to my family. I really don't show them how much I love them. My mum does everything for me, She cooks my dinner every night, she irons my clothes, she helps me financially all the time and she is always there, I think one day I should tell her I love her. I think she needs to hear that sometimes, I wish I had loads of money so I could spoil her and take her away on a beautiful cruise. I know mum's don't last forever but I truly would be heart broken and useless without her in my life. Wherever she goes I would go with her. Whenever I have kids I can't wait to teach them all the things my mum taught me. Always love yourself and others. Don't ever feel second best and always respect yourself. I love her so much!

I was seeing Aoife and Gloria a lot more recently and it was really killing me that the squad was back together now when I am moving away to study. Why? It seemed so unfair. I just took everyday and lived it to the fullest. I was dreading our last sleepover. I was off the drink for a good couple of months and

I was really enjoying doing outdoor activities with the girls and especially going swimming. I loved it! I wasn't even bothered that I was single, I was happy and content being single and being able to make my own decisions.

To cut a long story short I eventually got into Swansea University. I had to quit my job in Downpatrick, thank GOD as I couldn't stand it after our old boss left. Our new boss was a bit of a knob.

Counting down the days was horrible because I knew I had to say goodbye to my family. I am nothing without my family and always need them in my life I don't know how I am going to function in this life without my family.

The day came when I had to say goodbye to everyone. The good thing about saying goodbye to Ella was that I would see her again in couple of weeks because she was going to the same country as me to study! She was only an hour away which was fantastic! The whole family had a big chinese the night before I left. Of course I had my salted, chilli, chicken with curry chips. Around the table was my strong minded Auntie Geraldine, my funny yet loving Uncle Martin - WHO I LOVE! My amazing Nanny Dee, my annoying, yet caring, Sister Laura and my adorable Mummy! It was the final meal. I couldn't even look at my Auntie's face because I knew if I looked at her I would cry and I wanted to eat my dinner without gagging over it. The dishes were finally done and the time was near, I had to say goodbye. My uncle hugged me, and said I'll be okay. I trusted him. Hugging Nanny Dee wasn't too bad… I slept over at her house the night before so we had our goodbyes already done. I was hugging Geraldine and I just didn't want to say the words but I had to, "Goodbye, I'll call you when I land." I cried a bit.

As soon as I got to the car I CRIED my eyes out. I didn't want to leave anyone.

I got home and packed the rest of my stuff (well Mum did) and said my final goodbyes to everyone on Snapchat. I was wearing my tight, pink shorts with a vest, "Goodbye everyone, thanks for everything. Miss you all so much already! See you during Christmas"

Leaving the airport and saying goodbye to Mum was the hardest thing ever. Walking to security and watching my mum wave at me was horrible. I felt like she should be coming with me. I didn't enjoy it at all. It was a horrible feeling and even thinking about it now makes me want to cry.

CHAPTER TWENTY
New Beginnings

I had a great first couple of weeks being away from home. You get to party and have fun and of course I was back on the drink, which wasn't such a good idea when you're trying to make friends. I was living with girls who I literally would have done anything for, Brooke, Jessica, Meg, Gabby and Ellie. I really did love them. We had a group chat online months before moving in together so we literally knew each other so well by the time we actually met each other. I remember grabbing my keys at the desk and Jess came over straight away and said "Hello Ronan". I died! She was so pretty, cute and those eyes! I loved her accent. Her family were behind her and I got to see her family and hugged them all it was so nice. I felt so welcome.

Walking up to my flat for first time was so fun, I was so excited, getting to see all the girls. Brooke was so shy the first week, I just wanted to attack her to the ground and be like "Be my friend forever." Brooke and I got so close we would literally sleep together every night watching movies. I hardly slept in my room.

We would do food shopping together, go on little days out. I could really see myself living here for the rest of my life. As freshers came we went to all of the events, got super drunk and I usually got too drunk and always had to fall out with someone. I literally cannot handle my drink I shouldn't even be drinking! I hated doing the dishes, it was such a task.

As our lessons started I had to travel to Townhill, which was like fifteen minutes away from where I lived. It was a struggle trying to find the place. I was only a newbie remember. My first classes were fun, getting to know everyone, trying to find who I got on with more than others. I got on with everyone, especially James. James was my rock when it came to me needing someone. I was running out of money because I always spent it on drink. He would normally drive me home from my classes. He was such a cutie. I did have a little crush on him, not a normal crush. It was weird because he wasn't my type and everyone always thought he was gay. He was just always there for me and we had such a connection. Nothing ever happened so don't worry!

Life can never be simple when it comes to mine. There was always some sort of drama and it was normally always was my own fault. Why do I cause problems? I thought moving away from home was meant to be a fresh start for me but maybe I moved way too soon. I was in major debt. I had to start counting my pennies in my money tin to survive.

I could write so much about living with those girls in our apartment B24 but I would rather keep the good memories to myself as it was so special. I just wish I had met them in a different time in my life. I was back to my old habits, drinking during the day. I just couldn't cope. It got to the point where I had to move out of the apartment and find a different place to live because I just wasn't happy. Thinking about it back then it was all their fault, but really it was all mine. I wasn't at a happy place and my attitude reflected that. I miss them so much but moving out was probably the best thing to do. I was running out of money and I had spent all my student loan in the space of a week on drink and take outs. It was ridiculous, I had been able to get a job during the first week of living there but ended up getting FIRED because of my poor attendance and stupidity. Once I had actually brought a bottle of wine into work. Says it all, really.

Moving on, I moved out. I moved closer to my campus which was called Town Hill. Wow, wasn't that an adventure. I have been in Swansea now for about seven months. I was enjoying living in a new place. I got into my small little flat, oh my goodness, it was disgusting! Single bed, like WTF!

I never got to meet any of my flatmates the first day because they were all gone but the next day I was going to meet a very extraordinary girl!

My first morning waking up was okay... a bit cold but sure what can you do? I got my jumper on and made my way into my new kitchen and there was this girl with fuzzy hair, staring at the pan at the food she was cooking, don't even ask me what she was cooking because I had no idea. I was so nervous to say "Hi" but really wanted to know who she was and if she could be my new friend, haha.

"Hi, I just moved in yesterday" I said. She replied "Ah cool. I am Merran." I couldn't understand at first, to be honest I thought she was more German than Welsh. I had no idea what she was saying. It took me a couple of days to warm up to her and then we became friends instantly!

She is that type of person that comes into a room and you feel so much happier when you see that smile. I would have spent the majority of my time with her that month as it was just so much fun! I got to meet her incredible friends, Sara and Rachael. Sara has a baby now and Rachael is still the collect, skinny bitch you'll ever meet! Merran was my best friend.

We would cook healthy meals together and we would ask how each others days were after a long day in class! We would go out for nice meals, have enjoyable meals in and watch Brittany Murphy movies all night in bed! We would go shopping and just do really cool things! I was really enjoying being away from home for once, having a friend like Merran!

Could I really see myself living here for three more years? Of course something bad had to happen. I started drinking again but this time I ended up on a stretcher heading to the hospital. I took my medication late one day because I slept in, never thinking I was going to be drinking that night, but I ended up drinking two bottles of wine. You know what it's like when someone invites you out last minute! I ended up on the floor taking a seizure and the only thing I remember was waking up in hospital with all the leads in my arm!

My mum was called at like six in the morning. It was awful. I was on three drips and I am pretty sure my boxers were soaking! FML!

I was just so disappointed in myself that I had let myself get in such a mess again. I was doing so well in my classes but it was always in the back of my head, "what happens If I mess up again?" I just wasn't feeling my classes anymore. The good vibes turned into bad vibes and I was just getting so bored of doing the same thing all over again.

I don't know why I even travelled across the water to study acting. You don't study if you just have the talent naturally and I didn't really want to spend another three years learning something I already knew...and I really missed my family. I made the bold decision to return home. I was in major debt. I was costing my mum a lot of money. I had got on the wrong side of literally everyone I had met in both Swansea and home. Time to go.

The good thing I got out of Wales was making friends with Merran! I recently flew over and we had a weekend of laughter and fun. it was wonderful. She is actually coming over here for Easter which will be quite fun! Anyway sorry for getting off the topic there, I just hate talking about my failures in life.

CHAPTER TWENTY ONE
Home for good

Coming home, especially to a new house, was amazing. Mum had decided to move to the beach in Ballyhornan which was exactly what that medium said to me a year ago! The house was an old military camp house which meant it was all run down and old but still livable. Well that's what we thought.

I was back living with my mum and she wasn't so happy about it. I was putting the weight on which wasn't a good thing for once. I had already put a stone on during the time in Wales. I was so ugly. I kept coughing which meant I probably had the cold and I really needed to see a doctor but I hate going to the doctors since the whole rehab thing. I just didn't really like it. I called it off so many times. My cough got worse, I would wake up in the morning with constant nose bleeds and sore heads. I would self medicate. two paracetamols, two decongestants, two of my ADHD medication pills, one hayfever tablet and two spoonfuls of my cough bottle as soon as I woke up. I would feel a bit better for at least 4 hours. I was always a bit light headed and I had really bad heart palpitations. My body just wasn't right.

I did some research, which you should never do by the way because *Google* always tells you one thing, you're going to die. I hate you *Google*!

During those couple of months of horrendous pain I got a facebook message from a producer who found me on YouTube who was casting for a show about naked dating on the channel *TLC*. I was so excited after getting the message I called my mum straight away and told her and she quickly told me to apply for it! Of course I applied for it.

The good thing about being at home was that I got to see my family a lot more and also got to see Gloria and Aoife again! Oh and Gloria's first ever boyfriend, Robert.

They were all so excited and couldn't wait to hear more. As the days went on I got sicker. I started being sick in the shower during the mornings and before going to sleep at night. I still thought it was just a really bad bug but I couldn't afford to get sick especially before I was going to apply for this TV Show. I ignored Mum's advice about going to the doctor.

I applied for the show. The casting assistants got in contact with me during that week and we got on skype and had loads of calls and interviews and I even got my naked, fat body out on camera for them. I was 100 percent certain I wasn't getting the show. I was way too fat. I was so nervous and being nervous made me feel even sicker.

As that month went on I just had to go to the doctor because I was finding it too hard to breathe and I needed to figure out what was making me so sick. I walked upstairs in the hospital, oh my goodness those stairs killed me, my Nanny Dee could sprint up and down them twice and not even be tired. I am so unfit. I got into the room and straight away he noticed the colour of my face. He was like "you don't look too well at all."

He looked at everything, did some tests and he said "You have a serious mould infection." "What?" I said, "like moulded bread?" I hadn't been eating moulded bread. Oh, mould like the dampness mould you would find on a dirty, old, rusty wall. He said I was living in poor conditions. To be honest he was quite right because my room in Swansea was freezing and always had a big black mark in the corner of the room where I slept and after going to the doctors that day mum and I checked around my room and found the mould behind my wardrobe. It was so serious my lungs were clogging up with the bacteria. If I had left it any longer I could have died. I had to move rooms and everything! It was very dramatic in my eyes. We didn't have the money to get it fixed. I bled my mum dry as I had spent so much money in Wales. We were running out of money, well Mum was. Life was not good.

Things got a bit better when I came home that day and had a missed call from the producers of *TLC* saying they wanted me for the show and that they would fly me out the following day for filming! WHAT?!

Thank God Mum got to come with me. London here we come!

CHAPTER TWENTY TWO
London

The next day was so exciting yet so painful as I was still really ill. I ignored the doctor's orders and got my flight out and flew to London with Mum. I actually hated flying. It was horrifying. I literally think the plane is always going to crash every time. I hate it.

We arrived in London, wow this place is so pretty but so busy! I want to live here. We were walking out of the airport and saw our names on a small, tiny board, "Rowan and Trisha." How embarrassing... my name is RONAN!

We were driven to our hotel outside London a couple of minutes from the studios.

The email I got when getting off the plane said to "wear something nice to the studios with no makeup on". I had brought a couple of nice shirts and some skinny jeans.

We stayed in the *Holiday Inn*, nothing too fancy but the beds were so comfy and I was able to breathe, which was good. Mum and I were up all night in bed talking about what could happen after I go on TV for the first time, well second time actually.

I kept forgetting I would have to strip on TV, what the hell!

I had such a good day. I felt so at ease as I knew I was going to make good TV tomorrow. I was only nervous doing it on my own as this was the first TV appearance I would have to go on with nobody but myself as the focus. What happens if I fall or something? Haha, I hope not.

I finally got some sleep and woke up fresh as a daisy around 6:50am. That's pretty good timing for me. I got a shower went down stairs had breakfast and made my way to the studios saying goodbye to Mum. She sadly couldn't come with me but was able to stay at the hotel and relax.

Getting into the black windowed car felt unreal. I felt like a proper, important person. I got to meet one of the producers in the car on the way to the studios, got to know everything about the show, got the car parked and made my way in the building. It was the same studios where Cheryl Cole made some of her music videos. I literally nearly died with excitement!

I wasn't even nervous meeting all of these random important people that could change my life forever. I turned into this professional man who was hand shaking everyone. Walking down the long hallway to the dressing room was cool, "Hello you must be Ronan" was all I heard!

I got into my tiny dressing room which was filled with free chocolate bars, haribos and apples. I love haribos! I had like six bags and was still hungry. I got my makeup done by this lovely woman. I was then sent back upstairs and had a couple of photoshoots, one with my clothes on and one with my clothes off. To be honest when it was happening I didn't care how I looked. I was in the zone. I was in work mode. I knew I had to make it in this industry so I closed my eyes and counted to three and took my shirt off along with my jeans. I was getting photos taken for at least an hour. I was so tired but I knew if I showed any sign of weakness or unprofessional behaviour I would never get this opportunity again. I just sucked it up and got my clothes back on and then made my way upstairs for some interviews.

The cameraman was so hot! I just wanted to see his willy! Don't worry I didn't get to touch it. It was time to go downstairs to the studio. I was still feeling so ill I could hardly walk down the stairs. Walking into the main studios where we filmed the show was so dark. Stepping over each wire for different cameras and lights was so exciting but yet so scary. I tried so hard not to trip up. I was wearing my denim, skinny jeans and a bright pink shirt. I was hoping my sweat marks weren't going to make headlines.

I got the brief about what I needed to do and I just did it. "3,2,1 GO." I was to walk out to the bed on my own in the dark studio. All i heard was this eerie silence. I was so nervous but yet inside I was dying with excitement. Is this what my life is going to be like from now on? In my head I had a plan…..

1. Don't look directly in the camera.
2. Don't swear!
3. Don't pick your nose or smell your armpits.
4. Don't kiss on the first date…
5. Make sure you say funny jokes.
6. Breathe in at all times.

It felt like I was in this studio all day but it was only for thirty minutes. I was having so much fun but the guy wasn't my type at all. I think the producers knew that but wanted to spice things up a bit to cause drama. I didn't give them drama, I gave them me, the real me. Screw the top six things in my head. I did smell my armpits, I did kiss on the first date and YES, I did pick my nose!

I was so excited to watch myself on TV. I looked like a beached whale! I had to do loads of press work for the show, I was contacted by *Belfast Live* and *Down Recorder* for a photoshoot and interviews. I was being told what to say for each interview, as the show hadn't been released, but had some input in what I could say and not say so it was okay.

The newspapers published my story and everyone went crazy. I went to Asda one night and someone asked me for a photo and I wasn't even on TV yet! I was so nervous. I didn't have that big of a following anymore after I finished YouTube. What if everyone hates me?

The night came where it was to be shown on TV. I came across so well! I was so happy how they had edited it. They didn't show too much of my body. people were messaging me such beautiful things. People who were struggling with their weight were really inspired by me. I loved them! I love my fans. I know people can laugh when I say fans but if you walk out of your house and someone who knows you asks for a photo it's called having a fan.

People who never talked to me were now messaging me. Every time I went out I had to look good, I couldn't look bad. I felt like I had to put this image out that I was perfect and happy to help others feel inspired. That was my new job. As the show came to an end I was contacted by a producer on twitter, "Hey Ronan, saw you on *Undressed,* you were so funny. Would you be interested in having a conversation with us about a show launching on *Channel 5* in a couple of months?" OMG "YES!"

Was this actually happening, What did I do to deserve such good luck? During the process of auditioning for the new *Channel 5* show all eyes were on me everywhere I went. How embarrassing was it for everybody to see me naked on TV? Maybe I was just paranoid but most of the town already knew me from my YouTube Days so when word got out I was on TV it became even worse.

The *Channel 5* show sounded so big, like *Big Brother* is on *Channel 5*, imagine if I got onto *Big Brother?* After several conversations with the casting assistants for *Channel 5*, I found out that the show would be called *One Night With My Ex* and I had got the part!

I was casted for the first series and I would be on the first episode. There was a lot of talk about what ex they wanted on the show. They wanted to cast Freddy for the show but I really didn't want to work with him after how he treated me. They contacted Justin, and of course he said yes straight away when he found out he was getting paid for it. I knew straight away he was doing it for the money and not to win me back. What a loser!

CHAPTER TWENTY THREE
London

All that week I was stressing out, trying to skip meals, trying to fit in to certain clothes that just didn't fit me anymore. I had to go shopping for a new shirt because I felt horrible in all the clothes I had at home. I hated the way I looked. I was now wearing extra large shirts which is disgusting.

This time Mum wasn't going to come with me to London, I had to do it all on my own but to be honest I was quite excited because this was a big experience for me and sometimes you just have to experience these things on your own. Imagine me saying that! It helps you become more confident and smart. I flew over to London the day before filming. I was picked up at the airport, driven to my hotel and straight away I was nervous. I am actually going to see one of my ex boyfriends for for the first time in years! I kept thinking to myself, don't make a mug out of yourself Ronan... play hard to get and don't eat too much!

I got up super early that morning to get lifted to go to the apartments where the filming was taking place. I've never been to Chelsea before. Everything was so posh and fancy and the food was to die for. The most fun fact about the whole experience was that everything was free! Free food!

I got to meet the executive producers for lunch before my first photo shoot. He was lovely and he didn't particularly tell me that the show was scripted, it was just very well structured as most TV is these days. I was in photo shoots and interviews for at least three hours before entering the actual apartment.

The only thing I hate about working on TV is that the microphones are awfully awkward around the body parts. Because I was so big and fat the microphone kept slipping off because my boobs were jumping around the place. Ugh, I hate having man moobs. I wore a nice shirt, well I thought was nice, with black skinnies and nice boots entering the apartment. It was literally like *Big Brother*.

There was no camera crew there but it was all rigged up with cameras around the rooms of the beautiful Chelsea apartment. I could hear them move every time I moved my head. When I got into the apartment and shut the door I was in work mood but I was and am always very hungry, "Oh my God there is ice cream!" was one of the first sentences that came out of my mouth on the show. It was a hit!

I was in the apartment for a good hour before my ex knocked the door. "KNOCK KNOCK!" Yikes! I could not answer the door, I was terrified. What happens if it's Freddy and he tells me to stop eating? Too late as I literally ate half of the tub of ice cream in the space of an hour. I walked slowly over to the door and opened it. Bam! It was Justin and he looked so well, well that's what I thought until I watched it back on TV.

He was awful on TV, we were put in situations where we had to answer awkward questions. He was a completely different person on TV. He wasn't the Justin I fell in love with.

The whole time during filming I was just sitting at the sofa wondering why I had agreed to the this stupid show if it's only going to make me feel so useless and unwanted. I was overthinking it all so much. Will the viewers think I am stupid, will people call me fat? I had the pillow around my tummy for the most of it because I was so worried about how I looked.

It was such a long day getting back to my hotel around 3 am. As soon as I got in Justin texted me asking me to go back to his room for food…. Did I go to his room or did I stay in mine?

The following day was great, I managed to do some sightseeing around London on the big bus like a proper tourist. I love the big bus. I was also able to wear my fancy new coat. I felt so comfortable walking around London I just didn't want to go home.

The flight on the way home wasn't too bad. I don't really get scared anymore on flights which is so good because now I can enjoy it. I think I enjoyed London because I got to wear whatever I wanted. Back at home I would always have to look good if I was going out in public because everyone would bump into me and start talking to me. It's common sense to feel like you need to always look good in public.

CHAPTER TWENTY FOUR
Back to reality

Coming home from London was weird. I started uploading pictures from my filming (those that I could show) and my social media went crazy. "Oh my God you are going to be on TV again" "Are you back with your ex?" I was asked so many questions. I was really enjoying keeping people on their toes and entertaining them. All the support I have is incredible. I will always be so grateful to have you guys always behind me. I will never let you down hence why I wrote this book because I want every single one of you to know the deep, real me.

When I got home the vibes were off in our squad - Gloria, Aoife and Ronan and Gloria's boyfriend, Roger.

It was like Gloria didn't want to hang out with us. Aoife was keen to have a sleepover mostly every weekend, which is why I love her! Gloria was getting on like she didn't care about anything. It was always about her boyfriend. She would change how she acted when around him and just got on like a complete dick. I always said, chicks before dicks. That's how it works in my life, you never choose your boyfriends over your best friends. Ella had a boyfriend and she always had time for me, which reminds me, I can't tell Ella that Justin wanted me to go back to the hotel room with him, she hates him and would hate me even more if she found I went...which I DIDN'T!

The squad slowly turned into two, Aoife and I. I was okay with that. Aoife and I got on great. More than great...amazing. We would have sleepovers every weekend! We would go to Mcdonald's weekly, snapchat hot boys, go for long, late drives and most importantly, poop in front of each other! I was excited to see Ella though because she hardly gets a break when she is in Cardiff but to be honest I am so proud of her for always finishing everything. I should really tell her how I am proud of her. I am pretty sure she would love to hear it, for once.

Aoife and Ella have been there for me through thick and thin, I would call them mostly every night and I know they don't always vibe together but they definitely always try when it's the three of us.

I wish Ella was here to watch me on TV but she will watch it whenever she has the time. It was showing around 10pm. I know, so late. I was wrecked. I wanted the whole family around but everyone was so busy. The production team and promo team promoted the hell out of this show. My Auntie was in labour with her newest baby. While she was in labour the TV was on and the advert came on and she was like, "That's my nephew!" KEEP PUSHING! I love when I make my family proud, especially when I do my TV work.

As the big night came I was on the first episode, of course! I came across so well and I cried my eyes out. It was nice to be able to watch it with Aoife, Mum and my cousin Ethan, and of course the whole world as well, haha!

The day after Aoife and I had to go to Asda, some man came out of his car to let me know his daughter watched me on TV. He was acting a bit odd, trying to get a photo of me. Aoife and I were laughing our heads off as it just didn't seem real. One newspaper made it out that I got engaged to Justin after the show with the big headline "Engaged" and then another headline was "I turned really slutty." I was so annoyed that they would put a big picture of me on a newspaper and put a headline saying phrases like that. They really don't care what they write about as long as it gives them money. Idiots.

It was nearly a month or two after the show finished, I was getting so many offers to go on *Jeremy Kyle*. I was offered to go on that with Justin and they would pay for me to go on it, NOT A CHANCE! I was also offered to go on *Judge Rinder* which I was really close to doing until my mum said no to it. She always keeps me right. I was also offered to do *100% Hotter* but I found that quite rude, was I not good looking…

Big Brother auditions were coming up and I knew for a fact that I wasn't going to get on it. I didn't apply for it. Life after *One Night With My Ex* was boring, producers stopped getting in contact with me, people kept asking me if I was going to do anything else. I was a bit lost, didn't know what to do for myself. Money also doesn't last forever. I was becoming one of those people you hate where they constantly borrow money of you, it was embarrassing. I was living off my friends and Mum.

It came to the point where I had to sign on to the dole to get money. I was of course looking for jobs but it was literally so hard. Going to the dole was probably one of the most embarrassing moments of my life. No one really likes being on it. The hardest thing was walking up to the place, everyone clearly sees you and know where you are going then word gets around that you're on the dole. It was just unnecessary attention that I did not need! I would spend the money I get on chinese food, Mcdonald's, drinks, stupid shit that I just didn't need to put into my body. Mum didn't see any of it. I was slowly putting the weight on again. I was like a big giant pile of shit.

I was not happy with the way I looked and I wanted to do something about it but I just didn't have the confidence or motivation until the one message that would change my life forever.

CHAPTER TWENTY FIVE
Ugly

I didn't feel beautiful anymore.

I was the heaviest I had ever been, like you know you're fat when you get a stitch walking up the stairs. I was on my laptop listening to Britney Spears and I got a message on twitter. I thought it was going to be another pointless show offer but it wasn't. It was *MTV*! "Hi Ronan, well done on *One Night With My Ex* you were so great, I was wondering if you would be interested applying for a show for *MTV*?" Yes please, yes!

I applied straight away, was so excited just to write my name on the application. I even put a tiny heart beside it because I was so excited. I felt like I actually had another chance to turn my life around. Aoife was literally over the moon when I told her about *MTV* contacting me, well it wasn't *MTV* themselves but it was a production company, *Whizz Kid,* who worked for MTV. *Whizz Kid* make the show EX ON THE BEACH... I KNOW, right!

I called Ella straight away, she was blown away by it all. I kept it on the low down because it was still early days. This was around April 2017. I told Mum straight away when she got home from work but she didn't get too excited because she knew it was early days. I was so sure I was going to get the show. I thought that was it, everything will now run smoothly but no, I got another message! *Gogglebox* wanted me to apply for the show with my mum. Two shows in one day, wow, I nearly peed myself. I was so excited. I had to skype the casting team for *MTV* during the same week as *Gogglebox.*

I was so nervous because I haven't had skype calls in ages and I looked awful but as soon as they called me I turned into my usual bubbly self. I tried to keep myself busy while waiting for news.

CHAPTER TWENTY SIX
Friends and family

I went to Aoife's formal where I got to wear a red dickie bow. I really enjoy spending time with her like, literally, everyday. Ella was always my best friend but slowly but surely I had two best friends.If you ask me which friend are you closest to, I honestly couldn't answer. I love Aoife and Ella. They are there for me like everyday either on the phone or in person. I would be nothing without them, maybe even dead. I really respect their opinions and thoughts on life, they work hard to get things in life and they never get a break.

Ella was one of the first friends I ever had, and Aoife entered my life at a time when I needed her the most. They are so close to my family my mum would even hang out with them. My whole family have a lot of time for Aoife and Ella. I am pretty sure if I went away for a while (not that Im going anywhere soon) they would still come over to my house if I wasn't there just to see my family. I always said when we grow up I want to be a part of their lives. I want to grow a tight bond with their kids - Uncle Ronan.

I just can't wait to grow old with them.

I have a fish at the moment, Reggie. If he had babies, which isn't possible, but if he did I would call them salted chili and chicken... what legendary names! I love Reggie, he is literally my other best friend. I talk to him every morning, mostly about my problems in life. I am pretty sure he cares because he always does a wee dance when he sees my pretty face. My little Reggie, love you buddy! I might get another fish, I'll wait until Ella visits and maybe she could help me pick one. Her boyfriend, Joe who, I literally love, has loads of fish. He even has a big fish tank whereas I just use my mum's old halogen oven.

It was a normal day, I was in McDonald's drive through with Aoife up in Portrush when I got a phone call from *MTV*, oh my goodness! I answered screaming "HELLO", calm down Ronan, calm down. "Hi you, how has everything been?" she said. I replied "Aww really good I am just getting a *McDonald's*." Why do I say these things? She continued talking about how the producers from the show really liked my audition tape from skype and would really like to get to know me more. They wanted to skype my mum, Ella and Aoife the following day. I had to quickly call everyone to make sure they were free for the call and call back with *MTV* to confirm that they could do it. Surely that was good news if they wanted to hear more about me? I hope my mum is cool on skype. Oh Mum, please be cool!

The skype calls went great. I had to wait for another week or two until I heard anything back. It was crazy. I was literally having panic attacks every day when I heard my phone go off but it was only the dole. Jog on DOLE, I am busy!

I got a call back from *Gogglebox* and they were due to film around the same time that *MTV* would potentially be filming with me…

I had to choose, between *Gogglebox* or *MTV* and I hadn't even got *MTV* confirmed yet. I just made the bold decision to ditch *Gogglebox*. Maybe next year. It was nearly a month now,. Iit was late May 2017 and I hadn't heard anything back from *MTV*. It was the most terrifying month of my life waiting and waiting for a phone call. One night I was in the house with

Aoife, having a chinese of course, and my phone rang! Oh my GOD guys you will never experience the feeling I had, I answered it. The producers wanted me to come over to London to meet them. I was like "YES!" I was so shocked because I was having bad thoughts during the whole week about not getting the show but If they wanted to meet me then of course that's a good thing!

They booked me a flight from Belfast City Airport to London Gatwick then a driver would pick me from the airport to drive me to the MTV headquarters. I got my eyebrows done by my amazing beautician before I left. She is literally a family friend now and will probably be invited to my wedding because she has been up my nose so much. She knows everything about me!

My mum dyed my hair to cover some greys and I left for London in the early hours. The car picked me up from the house to the airport, all paid for. It was the first time I was actually nervous about doing this. I was meeting the producers from *MTV*. What was going on with my life, haha?

When I got to the airport there were so many hot men. There were so many emotions going through my head that day I just wanted to tackle someone to the floor and kiss them. There was one guy in front of me on the plane who literally smelt and looked beautiful. You know when you were younger in school and you would get your friend, Ella, to hit your arm so you would moan like a bitch to get the boy's attention - or Mikey's. Well that's what I did. I pretended to hurt my finger on the table and let out a bit of a moan. He didn't even look at me UGH. I had sit behind him for at least thirty or forty minutes. Thank God I was wearing jeans, if you know what I am saying....wink wink.

I got to bright sunny London, awh London I've missed you. I should really just move over here when I make it big. London is literally one of my favourite places in the whole world. I haven't been to many places but London is just so special to me. It was when my dreams became reality. I love you London.

My driver was so cute, he took my bags and everything. I had no idea what he was saying, I couldn't understand his accent but God I wanted to kiss him too. I am pretty sure I wanted to kiss everyone. If you are one of my many true fans you would remember him on my *Snapchat* story back in May. I am pretty sure the caption was "My driver is so cute." It was like a two hour drive to *MTV*. I really needed a pee. I just wanted to pee. I had to hold it in. I loved watching out the window while driving through London, it just made me think. Yes, I had a shitty childhood and maybe having an okay time now, but I knew if I worked my ass off to please the producers I could be living in London entertaining people every night on TV.

I drove past the big, cute clock, oh yes the Big Ben! I was just so happy looking out the window. I thought about a lot of things during that car journey. Imagine if I actually made it after *MTV*. I could maybe settle down and fall in love with someone who actually loved me. I am pretty sure the only reason why i was reflecting on life was because the cute driver had a really depressing radio station on and I was in the zone.

After two hours of driving I was finally in London. I was at the *MTV* offices! Oh my Lord!

I was dying for a pee, I didn't get to *Snapchat* much because I was struggling to hold in my pee, to be honest. I was a bit sweaty, like everywhere, because I was wearing a big jacket and London air is always a bit warm and sticky. I went into the offices straight away and sussed out the options for what floor to go to. I loved it.

I got into the right place, eventually, and knocked the door. A darling of a woman opened the door and was immediately kind. "You must be Ronan." What a darling. I was taken to the private conference room, you know the room with the big giant table with lots of chairs and cups of water. The cups had *Ex On The Beach* written on them! How cool was that. I just wanted to sneak one into my bag but I am pretty sure I would have been caught.

Suddenly two women came into the room and introduced themselves as the producers for the show. I got up and hugged them and said "thanks so much for inviting me over." I can't go into great detail about what was said in that room but all I can say was that I signed a lot of papers and had loads of photos taken of me. I was quickly sent to Soho in London after my meeting with the producers to meet a TV Psychiatrist, don't worry guys its crucial on every show you do. They have to make sure you are fit and well to be on TV and to cope with what could come out of being on TV. I was used to the attention and the constant backlash from being on TV, I thought it was going to be a piece of cake but boy wasn't I wrong. It felt like I was in rehab all over again.

She was asking me questions about how my childhood was, how my upbringing was. Have I ever tried to harm myself? I was asked so many questions.She asked me a particular question about not knowing who my real dad was. We got into more detail with that subject. "I always wondered what he looks like or if i have any other siblings." It makes me sad sometimes thinking about another family I could have had, brothers, sisters, pets, grandparents, aunties, uncles. It just makes me sad. I would love one day to find him and just meet him and maybe I would feel different about the situation. Maybe I would ask him why he needed to leave me at such a young age. It also makes me angry that he could have went on and started a new life with a new family. Was I not good enough for him? Would he be ashamed of how I turned out...? I just wanna know what he looks like. Is that too much to ask?

If I had the chance I would write him a letter,

"Hi, it's Ronan. Ronan, your son. I hope you remember who I am. I just wanted to write you this letter because I wanted you to know that I know that you left me all those years ago and never once tried to contact me to ask how I was. I am doing quite fine, well now I am anyway. I always wondered what you looked like and how you were with me? Did you ever love me?

I would really appreciate meeting with you someday just to ask you some questions. Do you have any other children? Do you love them more than me? Do you ever think about me?"

I would write that.

The psychiatrist also taught me how to address certain issues like talking to the press, talking to fans, being followed by fans and what to do if that happens. I never knew they gave you a full lesson on what do when you are on TV. As much as I wanted to cry in that room I didn't, because crying to me is a sign of weakness and I hate crying. Especially after seeing myself cry on *One Night With My Ex*.

I am such an ugly person when I cry. I was staying strong but surely she could read my body language. I was so uncomfortable answering some of the questions but to be honest, maybe I needed to talk about some of these things things while I was away in London. I did feel a bit better after talking about some issues I had in the past, about being bullied. I knew straight away that this show was going to be major big. I just had a really strong feeling about it. I was finally finished with this lady. She was sweet but she knew how to do her job.

So, basically, she goes back to *MTV* to let them know that I am either stable or not stable enough to be on TV or to be filmed. I was hoping that I came across okay to both the producers and herself. I was a bit nervous during the meeting and I was constantly talking about boys and food and they kept laughing so I am pretty sure they loved me!

I really didn't want to leave London, I wanted to stay for longer and just enjoy looking around and enjoying being free. I was driven back to the airport where I called my Mum straight away letting her know everything went well and I was on my way home. I was so hungry that I was going to get a *Burger King* at the airport. I did and it was great. I had two meals.

Following this, you now sit and wait for the contract to be sent out to you through the post. That basically means you are casted for the show! I was waiting around for another week before I got the call I was waiting on confirming that they wanted to cast me for the show! I was over the moon. I remember jumping up and down on the sofa like a little girl screaming, "*MTV!*" For once I didn't call Aoife straight away. I waited until I saw her next and was like "Say hello to the next *MTV* star!" I was so excited because I really deserved it.

I worked hard on TV. I always do. It took me a while to get it in my head that I was going to be on *MTV*. Like literally one of the most biggest channels in the world! There were rumours that the show would be international which means the show would be aired in all countries... woho!

I had to sign off the dole because filming was for twelve weeks and I wouldn't have time to sign on every Monday. I was so happy to be coming off the dole. I don't ever want to see it again.

I was so excited to start filming, twelve weeks is a long time. The show was going to be called *Ex On The Beach Body SOS,* a weight loss show but with an *Ex On The Beach* twist to it. It was going to be a big hit on TV. I started filming for it in June 2017.

The more exciting news was that Mum, Ella and Aoife would be appearing on the show during a couple of scenes while we are filming at home. They were also going to be filmed in Spain during my final scenes.

CHAPTER TWENTY SEVEN
Lights, camera, action

It was the start of June, and the day of filming finally was here, Ella was flown out from the beautiful city of Cardiff, back to Belfast for the pilot episode. Aoife was already sleeping over the night before so she would be here for filming the next day. Mum booked off work, bless her, and I was here, ready for action! I was so nervous! Two big cars came up to my house. The whole estate were probably wondering what was going on with all these people coming out with their filming gear. I was so nervous but yet really excited.

Josh, the director for the day, was so sexy, I always call him Joshy in a sexy voice to make him feel really awkward. I love him, then there was a runner Shane, lol. Shane was bit of an oddball but meant no harm. I was filming from 10am-10pm. It was going to be a very long day. I was so tired already but I knew work had to be done. I was being filmed at the house for half of the day then the girls were filmed, we had some interviews, and then we had to film at the local chippy. I had to order like 5 different meals and eat them all! I had no problem with doing that!

The camera was on me all day eating like a pig. I am pretty sure everyone from Downpatrick was writing Facebook posts about what was going on in town with the film crew... yeah guys, that was me. I was in the zone. I had no idea people were even around me while filming. I was just doing my job and didn't have any regrets. We finished filming our final scenes of that day in a local bar in Downpatrick. They closed off the bar for us to film. It was so fun because I got drunk really quickly and was loving life while Ella and Aoife were stone cold sober. It was really the first time I had both of my best friends in the same room at the same time. It was quite a cool feeling to be able to share the experience with both of them. I would do anything for those girls. I think because they have done so much for me now I think it's time for me to give back to them. I would jump in front of a bullet any day for those girls if that means they could live their life and follow their dreams.

As filming went on so was my social media following. Word got out that I was filming for MTV, after me stupidly posting a video of a scene from the local bar with all the cameras and lights in the background. Silly me... I do like to tease the my followers on social media. I hate calling them fans because they are so much more than that. They are literally family to me. I don't think, well I know, I wouldn't be here if it wasn't for all their cute comments under my posts and their ongoing support for everything I've ever done. I actually love them so much!

Throughout filming for MTV I was flying back and forth to London so much. I missed so many birthday parties, and nights out. I was so busy. It was nice being busy filming and working all the time. It got me thinking of what I wanted to do after the show is over...maybe get a part time job to keep me busy. I had to join the gym, it is a fitness show at the end of the day! MTV paid for me to go to the gym and have training sessions every day for the next 6 months. I was so grateful. That's where I met the hard working Roisin Torney, my PT.

The first day of my gym session was hard I walked in to the wrong gym like twice because I had no idea where this place was. She had nice blonde hair, well it was really blonde like a real sexy colour, nice pretty eyes and a banging body! I was like, wow, she is going to kill me by the end of this transformation. I told her everything I ate for breakfast, Pizza, chicken burgers, turkey dinosaurs, the whole lot. She was shocked and was like "We are going to change that straight away mate" I could tell she was down with the strict business and was going to whip me into shape in no time. She didn't want to be filmed which was really good for me. I got to have quality time with just her and was able to properly focus on my training sessions without having the camera on me 24/7. I saw her mostly every morning and she became a friend very quickly. Things were looking up.

I think on my next pay I will take her out for something nice to eat. I literally want to spoil her. She had everything I wanted, a nice job, a gorgeous boyfriend and a banging body.

During the first month of June I would be travelling to London a lot for photo shoots and filming. During this time I met some other people from the show but one person who I quickly clicked with was the most loving Paige Wallbank! A struggling mother trying to get her body back. She was so inspiring, She wasn't doing the show to be something to make money from, she wanted to inspire people like me and become something much more than just being famous. I loved that about her. We would call each other every day and night during the twelve weeks.

Filming for *MTV* was so hard, probably one of the most hardest shows I've ever filmed in my life. It was so structured, at the end of the day we are making TV, so it had to be entertaining. I was working with the likes of *Vicky Pattison* and *Charlie King* who had also been involved in TV work in the past and explained to me that this was nothing like they were used to filming. This new show was hard and it was stressful.

Some people think you just go on TV, film some scenes, be yourself and then you're done. It's so much more than that. There are constant re-shoots of the same scenes over and over again until we get the best one, constantly learning where to stand and what to do in that place and if you mess it up even an inch you have to start all over again. I was used to the stress and the work that needed to be done after the first couple of weeks of filming.

Ella hated it. Ella didn't really enjoy flying back home every month for filming, she didn't really sign up for that but she always stands behind me in everything that I do and that's what makes her my best friend. Aoife loved it, as much as me.

I started to really enjoy the gym sessions while I wasn't filming. It was my time off, no phone, no cameras just me working out with my body. It was hard filming in London because people are constantly taking photos of you while you're working and it's quite annoying. I had one really good day in London when I had to film in a dance class.

I had lost quite a bit weight now and I was doing a dance class in London near Soho. I entered a room not knowing who was in it, the whole point of this type of TV show is that you actually are surprised at some scenes they put you in. I was so tired because I had hardly any sleep the night before at my hotel due to thee fact that I got lost and didn't get into my room until around three in the morning. Anyway back to the dance class…

I walked into the room, there it was… full of boys! Not just boys… but GAY BOYS! I was having a dance class with a full on, gay dance company. I was in my element. They taught me

a real sexy dance and I was dry humping the floor, shaking my ass at everything possible that I thought looked sexy! I was having a little moment around this guy. He was in his late 30's but did not look like it at all! The producers kept telling me to flirt with him but I was so nervous, the best thing I came up with was "Are you single?" Who even says that? I just wanted the floor to swallow me up. I loved dance class. I felt something that I never felt before, the way I was dancing, I just felt so comfortable. Why have I never kept this as a hobby?
I remember my mum tried to encourage me to explore this years ago but I wasn't interested then.

After the dance class we all went out for drinks and a little flirt session. I am pretty sure I was asking all the boys for a kiss that night. Did I get one?...wink wink. I was in London for three days that week. I was so tired I just wanted to go home but I really enjoyed being around the gay guys. That was the first time I ever had a chance to get to know other guys like me which was really interesting. Filming with *MTV* happened so fast it was almost the end of July and it was coming up to my last two months on the show. I was informed that they would be flying me away again but this time for a full week in a place called Norfolk. Before that I had to be in London for another shoot and some further interviews. I had so much going on that week. I was so tired and they didn't let me get my eyebrows done or hair done because they wanted me to look extra good during my final scenes. So I was travelling around to a lot of different places looking like a mess.

I spent most of that week before flying away in my Auntie's with the kids. I love going down to see the kids, it takes away everything that worries me and I get to see the kids smiling which makes me so happy. I've taught them to call me Ronan Rice instead of Ronan, it's so funny.

I was losing so much weight that month and I felt really good. I really wanted to have some sexy time while I was away again in London that week because I felt good in my body so why not enjoy it? I messaged a guy I knew that lived around Norfolk near the hotel I was staying at. My hotel room was a mess. I had dirty underwear and clothes lying all around the place. I was in the hotel for two days you see so I was in and out several times a day getting dressed into something different. I can't believe this guy actually came over. We watched a movie, but we all know what happens during a movie... I felt like I was losing my virginity all over again. It was such a great feeling and I am pretty sure next door heard us. Sorry!! I had to video call my mum after it to tell her I got laid, she wasn't quite happy about it.

The next morning was so awkward, I was due to be picked up for filming around 8:30 am and he was still fast asleep at 8 am. I gently kissed his lips and said "wake up", nope, still sleeping. I even moved around the bed, he still wouldn't wake up. I coughed very loudly... Still didn't wake up! I had to get ready as I couldn't be late for my lift. I got packed and showered while he was fast asleep so I left a note beside the bed...."Hey, thanks for last night, I am pretty sure you were dead so I left without saying goodbye. Call me next week, love, your wee irish boy" but he never texted me.

I was on my way to bootcamp. Yes, fat camp, for a full week's training and filming. What a nightmare. I got to meet the rest of the cast members from the show, especially Paige! I was so excited to see her. Every time I tried and cuddled her she was like "go away, you melt." I just wanted some love, haha. I was filming for a full, intense week. I was drained, I was starting to break down. I had no phone, I was given food I would never eat at home and I was doing workouts by the hour. I was so drained and my personality wasn't coming across well during filming. I tried sneaking my phone in during filming on one of the scenes and I got told off. I just wanted to hear my mum's voice. I remember during one of our breaks I ran into my room and called my mum straight away. I cried so much that she probably had no idea what I was trying to say. My body wasn't used to having such small portions of food and I was literally making a TV show.

I was having a bad day but thought tomorrow is a new day. I woke up the next morning and was feeling refreshed. We went out on a hike to a gym where we would be doing boxing and stuff. I never boxed before, how cool! I felt like a proper man punching away at everyone. I felt the burn.

Bootcamp taught me that working out is actually fun. I really enjoyed it, I would love to go back but it's so expensive. All the famous celebrities go to it for like a month at a time. Maybe one day I can afford that. Maybe I should just stick to my P.T sessions with Roisin back at home. I couldn't wait to get home and tell her all the things I'd done while I was away. She would be so proud of me.

I was really excited to get home after that week. I missed the family so much and my head was so sore as well. I needed a good meal with the family. I was more excited getting home to watch all the shows I had recorded on TV. It's so hard to have a social life or some quiet time when you are literally on the go filming 24/7. I had a couple of weeks off filming. Aoife and I went for some walks to Cave Hill. It's a pretty big hill guys and plenty of other stuff that did not involve fast food for once.

My final scenes were coming up the following week and we would have to fly out to Spain. They booked Aoife, Mum and myself on the same flight and then Ella the day after because she was in Cardiff and we were in Belfast. I was excited to finish filming but also very sad because filming was almost over. I didn't want it to be over just yet. I was dreading it.

I was taken away to a different hotel when I landed in Spain. Mum and Aoife shared a hotel and I was in a different one due to filming. I walked up to my hotel, it was so shiny and warm. I loved feeling the fresh warm air on my skin, it was like a dream. I hadn't been away for so long I was enjoying the sun. We arrived on the Monday, and then left on the Thursday. I was filming from Monday to Tuesday night. Then I had two days off. Woho! Party!

I had so much to do, I had to get a spray tan on the day of arrival, filming lots of shots, interviews left, right and centre. I was doing sexy naked photo shoots with my fresh new tan. I felt good! The villa that we were filming at was to die for! It was magical and the view was great. I was there most of the day in my dressing gown. The whole idea of my final scenes was me coming out of the sea to surprise my family and friends with my new body. The girls would be at the beach later that day to meet me for the big reveal. The day was such a drag. They didn't give me any food because they didn't want me to look bloated. I had to sneak into the kitchen and eat an apple because I was so hungry. Meanwhile, the three girls were being wined and dined outside while I was stuck in a hot room.

It was nearly time for filming, to get my makeup done and can I just say, I've never met anyone so talented before in my life. The makeup artist, Natasha Lakic, was unbelievable! I instantly loved her as soon as I met her. Sitting on the chair watching myself in the mirror, I quietly thought to myself, this is it.. I made it. The feeling of her soft fingers and brushes on my nice tanned face was magical, I loved her. She made me look a thousand dollars! She lives over in London and we both promised each other next time I am in London filming I would go meet up with her. The hairdresser was a babe, but a babe with a girlfriend ugh. No way I was getting into his pants that night!

For the past twelve weeks my emotions had been all over the place. I couldn't believe this was my final day of filming for *MTV*. Walking down to the beach was so overwhelming, while I was walking people were fixing my microphone, touching up my makeup, telling me where I need to stand when I get to the beach. So much was going on but the only thing I could think of it was, this is it. This could be my last show, this could be my final day of living the dream. I have to make an amazing last impression!

Mum, Ella and Aoife were at the beach having drinks by the sun loungers. What actually happens on TV is that I came out of the sea and surprise them. How it works is that I am actually hiding behind a tent and pop out and surprise them. Standing in the tent, waiting for the countdown was the most terrifying moment of my life. I was baring all going out in only swimwear. I took my robe off and got ready to go, "3,2,1", it was my cue to walk. I walked out of the tent and immediately my mum started crying. Why was she crying? She made me cry! I gave her a hug and told her how much I loved her, seeing Aoife and Ella's faces beside my mum was such a gift. I had my three supporters all together. Then the director said "Cut!"

I downed a glass of champagne or two, haha. I recorded some interviews about coming out to surprise my family and friends before doing my final scenes in the sea. I was so excited. The sand seemed so warm but yet the water looked so cold. I was so nervous because it wasn't just a dip in the water I was completely in the water up to my shoulders. It was time to get into the water, a quick makeup touch and I was in the water. I blocked out everything in my head, I blocked out the crew, the press, the viewers and my family, I was in complete Britney Spears mode. I got into the water and Josh the Director said "Ronan, I want you to be the biggest diva when I start rolling." I replied "Oh don't worry, i'll give you all I got" "3,2,1, ACTION!"

I released my inner Britney Spears, flicked my hair, did a full dance in the water, splashing the water, listening to the crew and people on the beach cheer me on, I was powerful. I was on top of the world. All eyes were on me and for once it was for something good. I was so happy with myself. I'm pretty sure I splashed the cameras but hey, what Diva wouldn't?

MTV was officially over. I was no longer working for *MTV*. I was free. The first thing that came into my head was… LET'S GET AN INDIAN! I had two days to chill in Spain before flying back home. I was eating so much and felt so good not being filmed. I was able to have a swim in the pool at the hotel, was able to wear what I wanted, had some cheeky drinks with my favorite fellow co-star, Paige. Paige did so well, I am super proud of her. I can't wait to fly over and see her for a weekend. I love her so much!

CHAPTER TWENTY EIGHT
Take 2

What now? Since I was still contracted with MTV for another 6 months it meant I wasn't allowed to do any other TV appearances until my contract is finished. The good thing was that I had free time again, the bad thing was I had no money coming in. I had to get myself a job to keep me going until filming starts back up again. As soon as we got home from Spain I handed my CV into so many shops hoping someone would take me on. I really needed to prove to not just my mum but my entire family that I could get a decent job.

It was a month or two later and I still had no hope getting a job. I was worrying so much, then I had an email from a card shop for an interview. I got an interview for a JOB! I was super excited. Normally I would be shitting myself for interviews but I wasn't. I was so excited to get a job I just needed to come across well to my future boss. I wore a white shirt, black trousers and a coat. I got into the shop and said to the very nice girl "I am here for an interview." She took me down to the office. I was so excited. The interview lasted fifteen minutes. I had such a good feeling I was going to get it. I thought I came across just fine. She seemed nice and she seemed quite cool as well for a boss. I really liked her.

As the weeks went on I heard nothing. I knew for certain I didn't get the job. I even called them pretending I had a missed call from them to try and get them to think about me, haha. I was so nervous I wanted someone to believe in me again. It was two weeks after my interview and I was walking down the street probably to *McDonald's* and I got a call. I answered... I GOT THE JOB. Yes! Go me!

I was only a christmas temp but still that's pretty good! I'd rather get paid for something real than go on *Jeremy kyle* or *Judge Rinder* and be fake.

I started a week after I got the call. I was trying so hard not to be shit at the job. I pretended I knew what my boss was talking about so I didn't look like I was dumb. I would then struggle to do simple tasks. I knew I had to step up my game if I wanted to be kept on after Christmas. I made myself available to work every day. I wanted this job and I really enjoyed the company. I worked with all women, Tracy Beaker, the assistant manager who makes me work my ass off but still cracks a smile. I love Beaker, she buys me food when I get hungry. The amazing boss, Paula who at first I thought I was going to be terrified of her but have seen that she has such a kind heart and a hard working, strong, work ethic. She also has such a heavy flow when she pees, you can hear a mile away! I love that about her.

Laura, my baby girl, she is really my favourite, she doesn't doubt my stupidity, well sometimes. She always comes in with a smile and I literally love the way we get on together. I am pretty sure I want Laura to stay in my life forever. I have so many memories with Laura already and I only met her during Christmas time! She is so funny. I always get so excited when I see her walk into work. Lorna, the mother, I love how she makes me feel so at ease when I am struggling. She is a ray of light. She has so much to talk about, sometimes I think she thinks I don't care what she has to say but I could listen to her stories all day! Paula D, she farts a lot which is hilarious, some men treat her like shit and I think she needs to find THE one. She deserves a nice guy! Then there is Rebecca, my pizza buddy. She is really down to earth and loves a good WKD.

There is something about Rebecca that I want to get to know more about her. Klaudia, who I love, I want her to take me to Yo Sushi for the first time! Then there is Shanice. She pretends to hate me but I know deep down she jumps around in the office when she finds out I am working on the same nights as her. Sian, her makeup is always on fleek. she is also very beautiful without makeup and I wish people would see more of that beauty. We became drinking buddies recently and I can't wait to go out with her again as she has so much to give.

Working with the girls made me feel so comfortable. I loved working. I loved getting up in the morning and travelling to work. I was excited for Christmas. I was excited for life in general. I was slowly getting my confidence back while working with the girls and every day I had something to laugh about. It was the start of December. I had to work my ass off to prove to them that I should get kept on. I had to or I would be screwed. All the other temps knew what they were doing, well that's what it looked like to me. As the month went on I got more determined and hard working. I really was doing everything I could to be kept on.

It was Christmas eve when the day finally came and I don't mean Santa! I was finding out if I was being kept on. I was so nervous, I had a feeling I would be kept on but sometimes my feelings are wrong. I had to wait until the final 10 minutes. Paula was off that night so Beaker was in charge. I walked up to her very slowly, shitting myself "Am I getting kept on?" asked. There was a pause, hurry up Beaker, say something! She replied "Yes you are getting kept on, you eejit" YES!

2017 was my year! I finally earned something again that I worked my ass off for! I was officially a working man! Woho! Screw you bullies!

CHAPTER TWENTY NINE
2018

Now that 2017 is gone, I get to reflect on not only the amazing year but the wonderful life I have had. I was on *Channel 5's One Night With My Ex* then was approached by *MTV's Ex On The Beach Body SOS"*. Being ill from toxic mould but still being able to work my ass off on TV, overcoming bad habits, making new friends, making memories with people I love, finding who I am as a person. I am pretty sure my life isn't over yet. I am only 23.

I have decided to make a bucket list, so then when I am having a bad day I can look at this book and read about the exciting stuff that I will be doing in the future. I promise that I will succeed and accomplish this bucket list.

Ronan's Bucket List:

Get skinny again.

Find a boyfriend who loves me.

Film another 5 TV Shows.

Take my mum on another holiday.

Make new, exciting memories with my sister.

Get my own place or move in with Aoife.

Buy a really pretty rug for my bedroom.

Learn how to drive.

Spoil my family rotten.

Get married and have children.

Teach Happiness.

I think losing the weight was fine, it's definitely something that anyone can do if they put their mind and body into it. It's just hard to keep the weight off, like no one ever told me how hard it was to keep it off. After finishing the filming I did go a bit overboard and eat everything. I probably put seven pounds on while I was in Spain alone. My main priority now after filming is just to keep healthy and constantly make time for a workout. Everyone's body is different, you just need to find something that works for you.

I will give you some tips, drink literally loads of water, like everyday. You can never drink too much water. I love water. Stop eating junk food, fizzy drinks, takeout food and NO drinking any more alcohol. I don't believe in moderation because if you do everything in moderation your weight will go up and down and you don't want that. Have a cheat day once a month. Don't have cheat days during the week and don't skip meals. Make sure you have some money saved for personal training sessions. If you don't have that a personal trainer who is literally there for you every morning you will start feeling lazy and you need someone to keep you on top. Don't do it with your friends or family. As I said before, everyone is different and if you can't keep up with someone you will fall back so do it with a personal trainer.

Go to bed at a reasonable time, 9 or 10pm. Wake up in the morning at around 6 or 7am and don't eat anything! I think it is best if you get up in the morning and walk to the gym and do a workout straight away. You feel so much better working out when you have nothing too heavy in your stomach. Always walk back home from the gym, don't get a sneaky lift, unless you live in the middle of nowhere. Get home after a good hour's workout. Again I can't tell you what you need to do at the gym, everyone is different. Your personal trainer will know what to do with you. Get in the house from the gym and have some porridge with no milk just water. No sugar also! Or even some bacon and brown toast. Egg is the best thing you can eat but I literally hate it!

Enjoy your breakfast, eat it slowly and trust me... you will be so hungry after your breakfast but try and keep yourself busy until lunchtime. Have your lunch around 1pm and if you can't last that long have an apple or some nuts, grapes, greek yogurt, between the time of your breakfast and lunch.

Have a nice salad for lunch with LOADS of chicken. Chicken salad is the best! Put like, onion, cucumber, lettuce, sweet corn, bacon (cut the fat off) chicken, and remember NOT to use any dressing. I know it will be so hard without dressing but if you have chilli flakes that always helps with the cravings.

After a salad go out for a nice walk with loads of water, or do a wee dance in the kitchen like I normally do. Get Britney Spears on and dance all day!

Start making your dinner as late as possible. You don't want to be having your dinner around 5 or 6pm because you will be hungry all night and won't be able to sleep because all you will be thinking about is the pizza in the freezer. For dinner my favourites are prawn stir fry with loads of vegetables in it and always have some ginger, chilli and garlic in it as its gorgeous! Egg or rice noodles are nice with it as well! I normally have it with brown rice NOT boiled. Don't overdo it, only make some and have the rest for lunch the next day. Diet coke chicken is amazing or chicken and veg with baby boil potatoes with NO butter! Have as many vegetables as you want!

I am making myself so hungry after writing all of this. My main enemies are probably chinese and alcohol. You need to tell yourself NO! You can do it! I am literally so hungry now, haha. I think the most important thing about your diet is surrounding yourself with positive energy and people who are going to support you and join you. Don't let the drinkers in your life during your diet because they don't understand how hard it is to stay off alcohol.

What I learned while on my diet is that I found out who my true friends are. I actually don't have that many which is quite sad, especially now after being on TV. You don't know who wants to be your friend because they genuinely like you or if it is just because they are trying to get on TV.

Its my mum's 49th birthday today, so we are getting a chinese. I am pretty sure I haven't really been bothered with my diet recently but I am trying really hard to get back on the wagon especially before my show comes out on TV next week! I am so excited!

I am really excited this time because I am having a viewing party with my whole entire family, my amazing co-stars, Aoife and Mum, oh and Ella, through skype. My annoying, yet loving, Uncle Paul with his amazing kids, Corey and Hayley, I literally love them, I could have the shittiest day ever and get in their car and as soon as I see their faces I would start laughing. I love my uncle Paul and Auntie Louise, they looked after me while my mum was sick in hospital when I was born. That's probably why I am so close to them. My famous Nanny Dee will be coming she is literally so excited to see the show, hopefully she doesn't fart during it, haha. I hope she is proud of me. My uncle Martin is also hoping to be here, the funny bald man who always laughs at my hair but he is worse than me! Him and I got really close between this year and last year, I don't know what I would do without him. My Auntie Geraldine will be watching it, she never misses a show and my cousin Ethan. All his friends constantly ask him about me, the poor guy hears my name mentioned all the time. He loves it though and he is such a cool kid whenever he wants to be. My sister Laura will be coming down. This will be the first time we are watching one of my shows together which is so exciting! I literally can't wait to see her facial expressions, haha.

CHAPTER THIRTY
Showtime!

It was the big day! My episode is going to be aired! It was so crazy during the week. I had so many newspapers and online articles trying to find out about the show before it aired. I wasn't really allowed to talk to any press without *MTV* agreeing with it. I was approached by the amazing *Belfast Live,* they have written previous articles about me on my past shows and I thought I would give them a wee teaser of tonight's episode so I agreed to do an interview for them. Of course the sneaky *Daily Mail* had to steal the article and publish it in their newspaper the following day which was annoying because I had people stealing my words without actually interviewing me. *Daily Mail* also made me look so bad when I did *One Night With My Ex* their headline was *"I went really slutty"* with a big picture of my face on the page four! I didn't even speak to *Daily Mail*.

Well, anyway, back to my big night. The press was released during the day so everyone knew to tune in at 8pm! I was so excited. I was on my way home and I found out that the episode was going to be amazing. I was getting so nervous now. I hate being naked on TV! I had a plan, do a quick snapchat before it goes on and then turn my phone off because my phone always goes crazy when I appear on TV. I wanted to relax and enjoy it with my family! I was so excited! Ahh!

We all had a chinese, watched it, it was amazing. The feedback from twitter was fantastic. That's all I wanted. It meant a lot to me that the work ones watched it too. I really loved that. After the episode was over my family brought out a rainbow cake with some champagne. I made a wish when I blew out the candles. I am telling you guys the wish, it won't come true.

CHAPTER THIRTY ONE
The big city

I got a bit drunk as I drunk it way too fast. I had to be up at like 5.40am in the morning to catch a flight to Manchester the next morning for work. I needed to sleep. I didn't really have time to look through all the messages so I made a quick facebook status then I went to sleep. I was so tired.

The next morning in the airport was fun. I got noticed and recognised twice. Thank God I actually looked nice. I had to fly over to Manchester for an hour then flew over to the Isle Of Man later that day. I was noticed in the airport over there too! What! How weird! Was I really getting noticed all the time?

That week was so much fun. I got my hair dyed blonde, finally going full Britney Spears, coloured by the amazing Leighann Rea. She is so funny. She is my sister's friend. I love going to see her when I am getting my hair done. She gets me drunk and makes me eat nice cupcakes and stuff. I love the woman!

As the weeks went on after *MTV* aired my episode I felt so good about myself but I wanted to feel even better. I decided to do the one thing that I have always wanted, I got my lips filled while up in Belfast. I don't know why I did that! My lips were sore for days! I got a full syringe of filler in my top and bottom lips. They were so big! I felt AMAZING!

Anyone who knows me well knows I have always wanted bigger lips, the bigger the better.

I was loving life, being able to work in Belfast with people I love being around, talking to more producers about different shows for the future and most importantly writing this book! I wanted this book to be amazing. I worked so hard on it and I wanted it to be perfect. I wanted you guys to love it.

I auditioned for a show with *Lime Pictures*. I was so excited to fly over and film again. The producers were waiting for the channel to pick up the show but I don't think they ever picked up the show as I never got a call back. I did have other shows that I got asked to do but they didn't always seem the best tpe to help me continue to feel good about myself. The last thing I needed was negative attention when I was feeling so good. I turned one down because it was just not for me. I wasn't really interested in doing another TV Show. It was talked about going on *Ex On The Beach* but only if I kept my body in shape. Well wasn't that a failure!

I started putting the pounds back on again, I know, for God sake Ronan! It's so hard to keep the weight off when I was having so much fun with my wages. Food, food and oh yeah, more food! I was thinking more and more about moving out of Downpatrick and getting my own place in Belfast. Belfast just seemed so much more fun and you can do whatever you want up in Belfast. Like, I could go buy a loaf of bread looking like a tramp and no one would even judge. I need to move there!

I hadn't heard from *Lime Pictures* for a while, I hoped they hadn't dropped me from the show or anything. I would be heartbroken because it sounded like it was going to be a really good show. I actually emailed one of the casting assistants from my first ever show, *Undressed*. Jamie, she is called. She is amazing, I love her so much. She was a big factor in my life as she helped me get on TV and helped me throughout this whole crazy journey. She said that the show with *Lime Pictures* was actually dropped. I finally had some answers, but then that leaves me without a show lined up which is so annoying because I always like to have shows to look forward to!

Now that I am a full blonde with big lips, what else would I like to get done? Nose job, like I can afford that! My family, especially my Auntie, teach me to love myself and love how I look naturally but to be honest the society we live in today is one where it is really hard to have the perfect look and I need to get my nose fixed. I just don't like it.

As we were heading in towards Easter I was more and more determined to find my own place in Belfast. I needed to have my own place up in the city and I was itching to get moving. Aoife thought it was a good idea, yet she wasn't quite sure if I was going to be able to do it. That annoyed me a lot because I feel I have grown up a lot, especially with her and I always try to give her positive vibes when she has a great idea planned. I feel that we were getting more and more distant as time went on. It was getting to that point when everything was annoying us about each other. Yes, best friends fall out all the time but when we fight we say nasty things to each other and after a small fall out we took a little break. I think the break we had killed our friendship because when we started hanging out again, we bickered so much! We want different things and we are both going in different directions.

I am actually tearing up writing this because I love her so much and would literally do anything for her but right now… neither of us would be prepared to put ourselves out for each other. If you are a big *Snapchat* fan you would notice she is hardly in my snapchats anymore.

She helped me look for places to live in Belfast, there was just this one house. It wasn't classy, it wasn't clean but it felt just like home. I just wanted to be in it! I didn't even think about the pro's and con's I just wanted the house! I went and viewed it quickly and after leaving I asked when could I move in. That was the house for me.

Mum supported me, she came with me. I begged and begged and she finally agreed to let me move in! YES! I GOT THE HOUSE!

Sadly, the week I moved in, Aoife went to Canada to visit her brother so I didn't get to enjoy the first week of having my own place with any of my friends. Ella was busy moving into her own house with her sexy boyfriend Joe, congratulations by the way! Woho! Who would've thought that Ella and I would have our own places at the same time! Of course I got so angry that Aoife wasn't there but it was okay. I understood that she was on her own journey but I was disappointed that she wasn't there to share my new home with me. We had shared so much before and now I felt alone. Best friend? That was probably the make or break, it broke us. We exchanged several aggressive words to each other and that was it. We just stopped speaking.

Writing this today, two months later... I am not happy that we fell out but I am at the happiest I have ever been and I quite enjoy being on my own. I hope whatever she has going on in her life, she is enjoying it too. I will always have a place in my heart for her, she was my best friend and we had so many happy memories together, like so many! Aoife, I love you, maybe one day we can friends again but for now... let's get on with our lives.

Belfast here I come! I finally moved in, nearly died in the first week! I was making a very hot, chilli curry and had cut the chilli's but forgot to wash my hands after touching the chilli. I went for a pee, as you do. "OH MY GOD!" My willy was burning! I had to call my mum! "Mum my willy is literally on fire!" She told me to wash it with cold water. I am so silly sometimes in the kitchen! The curry was great though!

Living in Belfast was fine. I wasn't home sick because I was able to go to work and still have that familiar aspect of being at home, because all the girls I work with are like family to me. I enjoy being able to get up, make my own breakfast, walk to work listening to Britney and listening to my boss's heavy flow as she pees in the toilet. She has such a heavy flow I love it! Walking into work seeing my supervisors coat on the table gets me so excited because I know it's going to be a good day if she is in!

I have met so many cool people while living in Belfast! Wait until you hear about my housemates! I forgot to say that I moved into a shared house. I don't think I could live On my own all the time! I had to have some help and company. Let's go in order of the funniest!

Kyle, the good looking one from Dublin. He works on the *Game Of Thrones* set so he is super cool. He has his bike parked in the living room so when I get up in the morning I know when he is in or out. I love when he is in because we get to have fun in the kitchen, not that kind of fun! Play fighting, stealing each others stuff, running around the house. He was the first ever person to teach me how to work the tumble dryer. He is a legend!

Then there is Edel! That's not her real name but everyone calls her Edel. I love her! She is the first ever Vegan I have ever met! Her food always smells so good, I met her during the first week of moving in. We swapped each other's numbers and we became good friends. She does everything around the house, arranged all the bins and what goes into what bin. Her and I changed the layout around to make it more homely looking. She has a cool kid, a very bright one, may I add!

I think God heard my prayer on my first night of living here, "God, please let me have a great time here and let someone come into my life who will be there for me up here." Then, BAM! Edel knocks my door!

Jason, who also works on *Game Of Thrones*, he is super hot! I love his hair so much so that I just want to grab it and run my hands through it sometimes, especially when he comes out of the shower. He spends most of his time up in his room. I wish he would just sit with us one night and watch a really good movie!

Then there is Mark. He helps me out with all the bills and money problems. He is cute and caring and has a heart of GOLD! He thinks of others before himself and he knows a lot of things. I think he was in a routine before Edel and I moved in, work, lunch, dinner then bed. We changed how he lives. He comes out of his room now, he cooks with me, eats, watches TV, and even gets drunk with me! Well like twice so far.

Everything is good, only a couple of months left until my book is available on *Amazon*. I really hope you enjoyed reading this. I would be genuinely heartbroken if you stopped reading after the first page. I have never written anything before in my life so this is a really big deal for me.

My love life up in Belfast is weird. I have been dating, but nothing ever goes very far. I might as well just focus on my career than trying to find my Prince Charming. Work has been a bit stressful as well as we have been so busy. A young girl came into work a couple of days ago and she was so nervous, she came up to me "Hi, I was wondering if you are hiring during summer time. I have my CV here." Straight away… I had to look at the floor, I was going to cry! I remember how hard it was to find a job. Not so long ago I was that girl! I just wanted to give her a hug.

I was an emotional mess that day. I didn't know what was wrong with me. I kind of thought to myself while I was crying in the toilets, "Is this going to be my life?" I love working in retail and love being able to go home to my own place but will I ever be offered another show, after the book comes out is that me done?

I don't want this journey to finish yet. I am not even close to giving up! I had to snap myself out of this state and get back to work, get home and get emailing. I normally just get offered the shows but this time I applied! I applied for everything! *First Dates*, they didn't want me because I was on TV before! *Naked Attraction* came up and I actually thought about applying for it but then I thought, do people really want to see my willy on telly? Having my man boobs was enough but my willy… naaaaaah! That evening was just a disaster.

What I normally do is I pray to my Granda when I feel lonely and lost. I don't want to talk about what I pray to him because its really between him and I but it helps and I know he listens. I miss him.

The day after that I went into work, did my usual shift, 9-5pm. I had an okay day, finished work and headed upstairs to see a missed call on my phone! It was Jamie, the casting assistant! I quickly called her, several times actually until she finally answered! "Hey Ronan, would you be interested in a show about sexual health awareness?" "YES! Of course I would!" I love sex and I love TV! WAAAHEEEY! What could be better? The show was on TV before and it's coming back for a second series and I just had to say yes! Oh my God, there is a guy walking past my window right now with the biggest bulge ever! Back to the show... sorry guys. I have another show lined up! This is amazing! Another show, my first ever book and I just booked myself my makeup artist and photographer for my book cover! This is going to be such a good month!

The only thing I hate about living without my mum is that I have to do the washing all on my own, ugh, why does everything shrink? The good thing about living up in Belfast is that I get to see my sister a lot more than normal. We went out on a night out and Ella came with us. It was literally the best night ever, no drama or anything. We had the best night and it was nice to see Ella have a great time as well, for once! We never go out together so when we did it felt so good that we got home in one piece and we actually had FUN!

I love Laura, my sister by the way. She has good jobs and she knows how to budget. I need to learn a few things from her. I honestly couldn't have asked for a better sister. She bought me my first Hilary Duff CD and my first Hilary Duff movie! She has spent so much money and time on me I really can't wait to make it big in this career and buy her a big car and maybe even some botox! I know these would make her happy.

I am very grateful that I am close to my family, especially when I live up in Belfast now. My Auntie helps me out with my food and she is always there when I just need to hear a familiar voice.

People come into your life for a reason and leave for a reason. I am just glad I haven't lost any of them yet. I love them all. Ella is really family, she has been there for me for years. She comes to every family event. I really don't think I would be alive if she wasn't here. People say that about their friends but I honestly know I wouldn't be myself without her in my life. I hate falling out with her, it honestly kills me. I really do hate it. I want to be there for her through everything. I know she has a boyfriend who I really like, I kinda get a big jealous that I have to share her now but she has to have her own life and she gets to be happy and that makes me happy. Roll on the babies and the wedding!

I watched the Royal Wedding this morning, cried my eyes out. It makes me want to get married and settle down, I enjoy my own company and my own space but the way Harry looked when he saw his bride to be in that beautiful dress killed me! I think one day I'll find someone.

For now I am content with what I am doing now I don't really need anyone else in my life. I think I have enough. But then I think wait, I am 23 coming 24 this year and I am still single. Yikes! I don't want to be the old man on dating apps sending ugly, wrinkly, dick pics to young men.

I am talking to this guy at the moment who lives up the road from me but to be honest, I don't think it's going to work. I am the type of person who vomits when I see other couples kissing in public, no pda please! To be honest, if I had a hot boyfriend I would be kissing him everywhere! I think If I was a bit skinnier and fitter looking (I dont need to be fit, just look fit!) I could get a boyfriend quicker. It's a shame that a guy wouldn't like me for me, the way I am now. Why would I need to change my body to please other guys? I am happy with my *McDonald's* for now!

My mum asked me the other day in the car if I have missed Aoife recently. I haven't. I miss the company and having someone to sleep with during the cold nights but other than that I don't miss her. I do miss knowing someone loves me though.

Putting all of that in the past, I am quite looking forward to the future. I want to have a little rest from TV work. I have filmed four shows so far and have another one coming up. I think after I finish filming this one, during the summer, I am going to focus on other things.

I am also super excited for this book to come out! I am going to do a lot of work promoting it. I have newspapers lined up, radio shows, everything to promote the hell out of this book! I also hate doing TV work if it makes me look like someone I am not! That is probably one of the reasons why I wrote this book because I want you guys to know the real me. I am actually hoping to get some extra cash to save up for a nice apartment or flat. I enjoy the money I have but you always want more and let's face it, I don't want to be living with housemates all the time. I need my own place.

During the first month of June, a month before this book gets published, I decided to get back on the dating apps again. I ditched the blonde hair and got Leighann to dye it back to a nice light brown. We had the perfect day. I love going to Leighann's as she gets me drunk and always gets me in the party mode. I love the girls who work with her, I love the one who always washes my hair! She is so pretty! I can't remember her name ugh! Oh yes, I remember now Tierna! She is gorgeous!

Anyway back to me. I got my hair back to brown which I think really suits me. Everyone said it looks ginger but I am loving life! I look like Archie from *Riverdale*. I went home for that weekend to show off my new hair and most importantly to see my Nanny Dee. She is really into *13 Reasons Why* at the moment. I love being able to watch cool shit with her because let's face it... she isn't going to be here forever so I might as well enjoy every minute I have with her. We always have a routine when I sleep over. We have a small sized dinner and a cup of tea and watch something boring on the normal channels then when the sun starts going down, we close the blinds, get the pizza on and get *Netflix* up and running. We would sit up all night and watch movies. We are rebels then we are super tired the next day because we are up at all hours watching TV.

During the weekend at home I got to go back to Mum's house. I was looking through the calendar and guess what popped up.... AOIFE'S BIRTHDAY!

I wish I didn't see it because to be honest I wasn't really thinking about her that often. Well that is a lie I would think about her a lot. I got home that night back up to Belfast. I hated myself for looking at that stupid calendar. Her birt was the next day so I decided to write a cute post on Facebook about her and about how we aren't friends anymore. Just something nice to make me feel a bit better. As soon as I posted it, so many people were messaging me. I got so many likes and comments and before you knew it Aoife messaged me! I was like WTF!

I didn't know what to say, her message was "Hi"... I replied "How are you?" It was the most awkwardest conversation I've ever had in my whole entire life. I would rather talk about sucking dick to my Nanny than have this conversation with Aoife. We talked, we sorted a couple of things out and that was it. It felt like we never fell out, we explained to each other how much we miss one another. She missed my annoying feet in the middle of the night, I missed her texting boys beside me. I also missed our weekly baths. It was nice having her back in my life, well having her on the phone for now was good enough.

During the first week of June, I had so many things going on. I was struggling in work, like big time. I wanted to walk out and never come back, I also had a date with a guy called Aaron. It was a really good date! He picked me up from my Belfast house and took us for tea and coffee at a drive through. We couldn't sit in anywhere because it was quite late and he just got back from Seattle. He is a flight attendant. I know, how sexy! He isn't the typical gay guy you would see. He is nice and kind and has an adorable accent. I love listening to him ordering coffee. I had tickles in my willy and my heart. We kissed, that's all! I didn't suck him off or anything. I was on my best behaviour. I was working the day after and I got to tell everyone about my date.

I am getting super close to Rebecca recently which is weird because I never really understood her at the start until we went for a couple of drinks together and I just fell in love with her. We all go through hard times and it's nice just to let your guard down and hear other people's problems. You are either going to have really bad days in work or really good days. You just need to be ready to face whatever you are going to get but when you get a good day, that day is great!

I just need to remind myself sometimes that not many people have jobs so I need to respect that I have a job and enjoy it. We all just booked our Christmas DO! I am super excited. We are going to get all glammed up, drink loads of champagne and have lots of food! It will be weird seeing all of them out of their uniform, especially Paula and Lorna.

As I said you have really good days or proper bad days and today was a real bad day. Everything was going wrong. My housemates kept throwing little digs at me that would upset me. I was doing the complete opposite of what I was doing in University. I waited until my housemates went away home for the nights when I went out, I never had anyone around, I kept the place clean and tidy but yet that wasn't good enough. I was having to defend myself for every single problem that was happening to the house. I know I have fallen out with loads of people in the past but I sat in my room and actually thought.. "I'm I the reason I keep falling out with people. Is it me?"

I was trying to find a nine to five job so I could afford a nicer place. I was writing this book as well as trying to seal a deal with a TV Show. I was just up to my eyeballs trying to have the perfect life.

I confided in my friends and family and they thought it would be easier to save money if I was living back at home. That meant I would have to move from Belfast and start back in Downpatrick again. Did I want that? Was I going to pack everything up and move back to where it all began? I was. I had too.

I didn't feel happy anymore living up in Belfast. I was gutted because I met so many people and did so many things. I experienced my first bank holiday drinking day, I got to stop at *Cafe Nero* for my morning tea while walking to work. I met so many cool people at *Limelight*. I was able to work not just in ForestSide but also in the City Centre. That's whenever I met Shannon and Amy. I always have fun and feel myself when I am with them. I was able to book and pay for my sister's birthday dinner and surprise her with birthday cake!

The list could go on and on. I loved Belfast! My health and happiness came first so I needed to move back home where I could rebuild myself and find myself again. Of course I wrote a little facebook status. Everyone feels better after a facebook status. Thankfully Uncle Paul was able to help me move, I really don't give him enough credit. He is so kind and puts everyone first. I love you Uncle Paul! I actually bought him a father's day card, I can't wait to give it to him.

CHAPTER THIRTY TWO
Happiness

The good thing about coming back home is that I can see the kids more often. People have a saying that it's nice to have the kids in your life but it's also nice to hand them back. I hate that saying. I know I do get a bit tired when I am around them but when I am around them I am so happy. I love seeing them laugh and asking for me. I can't wait for them to grow up so I can show them all the photos I posted of them on my *Instagram*. They are gonna love it!

I don't want to go back home and fall back into my old ways again yet silly me went out with my old friend Laurie and got pretty drunk after a jog. I know, what was the point of the jog?

Laurie has been a good friend to me on and off over the past five years. I should start seeing her more often especially when I don't have Aoife anymore. Laurie and I get on really well so I don't know why we aren't best friends. She is also loaded so we could have avocado in fancy places everyday!

I came home with my eyes looking out for everything. I am keeping all my options open. I am thinking more about full time jobs than TV work at the moment. I just need something that's going to get me a nice house and help me build a future for my future kids. I don't really care if I am in a relationship or not I will have kids by the time I am 30.

I want to have cute play dates with Ella and her kids. I want to be able to dress up my son in cute clothes and post about it on social media and get loads of likes. I want them to dream big and reach for the stars in their dreams. I am quite scared in case Ella starts having kids soon. I want to be able to have our kids around the same age so they can be besties like we were, but before all of this can happen I have to make a living and save up!

I need to ditch this weight and start looking the part for TV roles. I need to get these lips topped up and get my wrinkles sorted. I don't have major wrinkles but I hate my crows feet when I smile or laugh. I just look ugly. A little bit of botox will do the job for that! I have it booked in for the end of July. Oh yes baby!

I am staying positive these days living at home. I have to or I'll fall back into my old ways again. I need to feel my inner Britney Spears again. I shouldn't be relating to Brittany Murphy, she's dead. I love her but I need to focus on the strong Britney who I aspire to be like more and more each day.

A lot of people said terrible things about Britney and she wasn't always liked. Look at her now bitches!

That's how I feel. For all those comments and situations where I was made to feel worthless, all those negative vibes and laughs directed at me. I'm here now, where I want to be, living the dream.

Twenty six days until the book release! I am literally so nervous. Everyone is going to know literally so much about me. Well, most things. At least you don't know how big my willy is!

My life is getting started again with the upcoming release of this book. A lot of journalists follow me on social media so they have been in contact with me for some press work. I am quite excited to do press work for the book because I don't have a TV channel telling me what I can do or say. It's all about me.

I am excited to explain what this book is about and what it means to me. I have been trying to slim down a bit as my photoshoot is coming up for the book cover. I will probably have to do a close up.

I have just spoken to the *Down Recorder*. They are the local paper of Downpatrick. They have been there for me since day one! They have always written nothing but nice things about me and I am quite excited to see what they have to say next. They have been very supportive. My Granda would be so proud of my write ups.

During this busy week I have been offered to speak with some producers for another show. I always get a bit stressed talking to producers because I always want to make sure I am free. If they give you a date and time you always have to say yes. The number one rule is to always say YES! If you are busy that day then get out of whatever it is that is making you busy because you only have that one chance to talk to the producers and you can't mess it up! I am also doing some press work for *Belfast Live* and *Belfast Telegraph*. I didn't agree to do any shoots for any newspapers as they always make me look massive, well more than massive.

The most exciting thing about this whole experience is that I get to share it not just with my family and friends but with Aaron… THE GUY I AM DATING!

I know, I know. I have kept this very quiet but if you follow me on instagram you will notice in two photos so far that I am actually with a guy. I was being really sneaky. I have never posted what he looks like, only his cute watch and sexy hand.

The first date we went on he took me to *Starbucks* for a nice cool drink. I had such a great time. We talked all night about everything and anything. The second date I took him out to my house and we watched TV with a cup of tea. We also shared some private experiences in the bedroom, wink wink. He is a flight attendant so I don't get to see him that often but when I do it's good. I like that he is away working. I get a bit weird when I see guys too much. I like to have my own space. Like I enjoy being home alone scratching my ass watching Love Island in peace. He is totally fine about what I get up to and what I do. He helped me out with a situation this week and gave me nothing but positive advice. I really needed to hear it.

I have been living in Downpatrick for 2 weeks now. I have been reunited with Laurie again. She is that type of "Feck it, let's go" kind of friend. She is always up for anything. I can't wait until I get paid so I can take her out on a crazy night out or maybe just buy loads of food. Both make her happy.

We get on like best friends but just don't call each other best friends. I think we need to work on a lot of things and be there for each other then maybe through time we could become closer to one another. I love her, she is trying to get skinny and is trying to make me do it with her. I am just not motivated for that shit right now. I am enjoying the fried chicken too much! We went out for a couple of nights this month and it has been super fun! I am actually in the mood to go out tonight now with her now. Should I call her?

The night is always great until we both get to that stage where we can't look after each other because we are both gone. I always end up going off with someone in search of pleasure, if you know what I mean! I really need to stop doing that. I am such a slut, now that I am seeing someone AKA Aaron. I won't have to do that anymore, only with Aaron, forever and ever! I can hear the wedding bells already people! Everyone is invited! I can't until Ella comes over so I can tell her all about him. I can just imagine the wedding right now.

I feel a bit lost some days though. I have always dreamt about being on TV, having it all. I have achieved that dream but I don't really know what to do now. I fell so bad for saying this but like is this my life over now? Are there greater things to come or is this it? I am bit confused about what's next. I get so emotional thinking about where I am in life because I had such a horrible time when I was younger. I didn't want to think about growing up because I thought life would be much harder and horrible.

I have now grown up and I am still alive. I am so grateful I didn't give up during school. There were days in school when I just wanted to end it all. I didn't care what my family would have felt. I didn't care how much it would hurt me. I just wanted to die. I am at a place in my life now where I can reflect on how I felt all those years ago and teach others, that there is light at the end of the tunnel. No matter how hard work is, how hard your parents push you, how hard school is, how hard life is on you, you should never give up. Your dreams will come true eventually you just need to wait it out and deal with issues and personal struggles before you find that happiness.

Nobody had the time for me, nobody wanted to get to know me and I felt so lonely. I have a big following now, with so many people looking out for me. I can't give up now, I have to keep reaching for the stars. I sit here in my bedroom writing this book, wiping the tears from my face, hoping one day you get to follow your dreams and forget about all the horrible things that have happened to you. We are all beautiful and we can get through this.

As I said before, what is next? I would like to film more shows, maybe write another book, after getting married, having children, buying a big house. Treating my family to things and showing them love that I wasn't shown. I want to teach my own children the importance of loving yourself, because there will be days when they don't. I want to show my husband that I am faithful and trusting in our marriage. I want it all. I just need to get there first. It might be another struggle to overcome but hey… it will be a piece of cake.

Love you!
To be continued..
Ronan x

Printed in Great Britain
by Amazon